THE GOD PICTURE

REVEALING THE MYSTERY WITHIN GOD'S NAME

Endorsement

"Greg is a true friend to Israel and the Jewish people and has been a faithful partner with the Fellowship for years. We are so grateful for his caring, loving support of the Jewish people in need."

—Yael Eckstein
President
International Fellowship Of Christians and Jews
www.ifcj.org

THE GOD PICTURE

REVEALING THE MYSTERY WITHIN GOD'S NAME

Gregory Martz

THE GOD PICTURE
REVEALING THE MYSTERY
WITHIN GOD'S NAME

ISBN: 979-8-9883965-0-5 Paperback
ISBN: 979-8-9883965-1-2 eBook
ISBN: 979-8-9883965-2-9 Hardcover

Contents

Acknowledgements

The first acknowledgment is to YHVH for inspiring me and revealing to me the content of this book.

The next goes to family: Jess, for proofing the entire manuscript with me, word for word. To Lilly and Milly for inspiring me every day. To my sister, Beth, who provided guidance and encouragement.

I send love to the friends who supported the project: to Rob, who suggested I put my research in book format. To Gary, who spent an entire red pen sharpening the manuscript. To Emily and Tim, and Angela and Phil, for support and feedback. To my friends Kenny, Joey, Jimmy, Kev, Marc, Jeff, Omar, Randy, Mikey, and Scott, for studying the Word and drinking coffee with me every Wednesday.

To Dr. Joe and Terry for walking with me through the process.

To Josh for his hard work on the audiobook.

Finally, to Brad and Hilton for their hard work and guidance throughout the entire process.

Introduction

I have felt a deep connection to the land of Israel and her people from a very young age. The Word of God says that the Land of Israel is a place that the LORD's eyes are continually upon. It was always my dream to visit Israel, to feel her sand in my toes, to smell the smells, and to breathe the air. A piece of my heart will always belong to Israel. At the encouragement of my wife, to whom I will forever be indebted, I took a journey to the Holy Land that would change me forever. When I boarded the plane for Israel in New York, I was a strange combination of exhausted, excited, and terrified. As the plane descended from the clouds and drifted over the coast of Israel, my eyes took in their first real glimpse of the Holy Land—I just knew something big was going to happen. It did, and this is the story.

I had been in Israel for a few days now, and something odd was happening inside me. After about seventy-two hours, my adrenaline from the last seven years of non-stop work was beginning to wear off. I was 6000 miles away from home, so there wasn't much I could do but just be. I rose each day and spent twelve to fourteen hours studying the Bible and walking the land where it all happened. One afternoon our Bible teacher walked us into the Jordan River to teach us about *Mikveh*, or ritual cleansing. This is the practice of washing the head, hands, heart, and feet before God. I had never heard of it before. I knew there was more of God than I was experiencing, but I didn't know how to find it. I knew that the fear-based, performance-driven religious experiences of my past were not the essence of God's love. I walked into that river broken. I stood there quietly, by myself, and said one of the most honest prayers I have ever uttered. "God, I know there is more to the Christian life than what I have right now. How do I get it?" At that very moment, a fifty-foot tidal wave crashed over me. When I opened my eyes to see the destruction, it was calm and sunny, and the brook was bubbling. I heard in that moment, "Close your eyes, Greg, it's Me. Let My Spirit wash over you." So, I did.

A few days later, on a sunny spring afternoon following a long day of hiking and studying, I was sitting on the slopes of Mount Gilboa, overlooking the Rift Valley in Israel. Having settled into my spot on a nice comfy rock, our rabbi started teaching from Deuteronomy. As I listened to his message, something moved deep inside of me. I had one of those moments that would change me forever. To make sure we're beginning from the same page, let me remind you what Deuteronomy 17:18-20 says:

> [18] Now it shall come about when he sits on the throne of his kingdom, he shall write for himself a copy of this law on a scroll in the presence of the Levitical priests. [19] It shall be with him and he shall read it all the days of his life, that he may learn to fear the LORD his God, by carefully observing all the words of this law and these statutes, [20] that his heart may not be lifted up above his

countrymen and that he may not turn aside from the commandment, to the right or the left, so that he and his sons may continue long in his kingdom in the midst of Israel.

In this passage, God tells His people that when a man becomes king, he should write a copy of the law with his own hand. Just a few days earlier, I had seen a man in the synagogue on top of Masada peacefully scribing the Torah and noted the practice as odd. Now, something inside me clicked.

When I heard our teacher reading this powerful instruction to new leaders, I winced and thought "Wow! I'm really struggling to lead well right now." You should understand that at this point in my life, I was leading at a level well beyond my own capacity and making a ton of mistakes. Listening to this teaching now, I could not deny it. Hearing those words read aloud, I knew if anyone needed to act on what was being spoken, it was me.

If copying the law by hand was vital to the leadership development of a king, I felt certain it could also be beneficial to a struggling technology entrepreneur like myself. I knew I had to try it because this was direct wisdom from God. It seemed so simple and frankly counterintuitive to me. In the age of word processing and voice texting, sitting down and blocking out the world while you quietly scribe the scriptures is something I would not have normally done. It is, however, one of the most succinct passages in all the scriptures on leadership development.

When I returned home from Israel, I began writing the book of Deuteronomy using pen and paper. It was old-school, yet somehow felt holy and calming to my soul. Deuteronomy was the obvious place to begin since it was the book that contained the command to write a copy of the law. As I copied the words of Deuteronomy, I noticed the phrase "The LORD your God" kept coming up. I must have written it hundreds of times. The more I wrote it, the more I became fascinated by the phrase. As a result, I began digging into the meaning behind it. As I wrote the phrase over and over, I noticed that I started writing it more slowly and reverently. To make it stand out, I would write it completely capitalized. Then I began underlining it. Looking back over my original copies, I could see the phrase everywhere, almost lifting off the page. Something was happening. Like a morning haze chased away by the light, the fog was lifting from my eyes. There is something special—something spiritual, powerful, and mysterious about this phrase.

I wrote the Bible for a good while as my personal devotional time, maybe a few years. First, I wrote Deuteronomy, then Romans, James, and several others. I began to leave notes for my children and future generations in these manuscripts. As I persisted, God began to give me clarity to understand His Word, and I began a journey to unveil the mystery of His name.

> *The mystery I began to understand is that the God who created the universe has a name.*

It didn't happen all at once, but slowly and over time. I began to dissect the phrase "The LORD your God." I studied the Hebrew, the history, and the usage of this phrase. I came to discover that the English word "LORD" is a translation of the Hebrew word "YHVH." This Hebrew word comprises four characters, YOD, HEY, VAV, and HEY. I studied the usage of this phrase and when and where in the scriptures it first appears. The mystery I began to understand is that the God who created the universe has a name—a singular proper noun that describes the essence of God! The same way I am Greg Martz, the LORD your God is YHVH. While we may refer to God by many descriptive names, God only has one true name, and this name has meaning so deep and so rich that it will take the rest of this book to scratch the surface of it.

Over my fourteen-year journey to understand the phrase "The LORD your God," the Holy Spirit revealed something amazing to me about God's name that has changed my life. Sharing these revelations with you is why I wrote this book. As we unveil the ancient mystery of God's name together, use these truths as a foundation and something new and sturdy to stand on. You are loved.

Words Are
Older than Dirt

According to the Bible, words existed before the universe. Take a moment and consider how amazing that is. From the very beginning of the Bible, we see God speaking: "Then God said, 'Let there be light'; and there was light" (Genesis 1:27). From the beginning, God is communicating verbally. God spoke a desire for light, and there was light. Proverbs 18:28 says, "Death and life are in the power of the tongue, and those who love it will eat its fruit." God created all there is by speaking. God employs language; thus, in its perfect form, it is holy and divine. How often do we think about the reality of God using an actual spoken language?

Before the fall of man, God would speak face-to-face with Adam and Eve. We know from scripture that they would take walks through the garden and talk. God not only created language but also used it when communicating with creation. This wasn't telepathy or the LORD planting thoughts into the minds of men. There was literal and verbal communication between them in a literal and verbal language.

> ⁹ Then the LORD God called to the man, and said to him, "Where are you?" ¹⁰ He said, "I heard the sound of You in the garden, and I was afraid because I was naked; so I hid myself." ¹¹ And He said, "Who told you that you were naked? Have you eaten from the tree of which I commanded you not to eat?" Genesis 3:9-11

Not only does God communicate verbally, but God is the origin of the written word as well. In fact, in this book, I will make the case that God's written word is original, concrete, and divine. That God speaks and writes may seem obvious since the LORD is all-powerful, but how often do we think about such a reality? You will soon see how important it is to grasp the concept that God created language, spoke it, and wrote with it. From the beginning, God desired to communicate with us and created language and script as the vehicle to do so.

We find the first example of God's writing in Exodus 31:18, "When He had finished speaking with him upon Mount Sinai, He gave Moses the two tablets of the testimony, tablets of stone, written by the finger of God." God wrote on stone tablets using His finger, and He wrote in a language Moses could read. For now, just keep this fact in the back of your mind—for later that this scripture references the very finger of God and that the finger of God is at the end of the right hand of the Father. Now, when God meets with Moses on top of Mount Sinai (also known as Horeb), He writes the Ten Commandments with His finger into the stone tablets, and eight times in the Ten Commandments, the name of God is written. God writes His own name down eight times. Moses subsequently had firsthand experience with the writing style of God. He had firsthand experience with how God represented His name, meaning Moses met with God, and he saw God's writing style. He saw the hand of God writing God's very name on the tablets of stone. Keep that in your pocket; this will become very important later.

Note that since language and script are divine, there was a common tongue between God and creation. They could speak and write to each other. Further on in the Old Testament, in the book of Daniel, we again see God writing in a language that man could recognize: "Suddenly the fingers of a man's hand emerged and began writing opposite the lampstand on the plaster of the wall of the king's palace, and the king saw the back of the hand that did the writing" (Daniel 5:5). As we read on in this story, we find the king was terrified by what he saw. It's not every day one sees the very hand of God, much less that hand, writing as a man does. Still, God's hand shows up again, writing in an understandable language on a stone or plastered wall. The idea that we as men would simply apply our finger to stone and produce writing is unheard of, but God does it with ease.

In the "fullness of time" Jesus came to Earth as God in human form. Did you know He also wrote? Sure, He learned to read and write as a child but was there something deeper? Something that showed His divinity? Remember the story of John chapter 8, the woman caught in adultery? When the Pharisees wanted to stone her, Jesus calmly knelt and began writing on the ground . . . but was it in the dirt? I can't claim the following as doctrine but humor me for a moment. When they brought the woman to Jesus, He was teaching on the Temple Mount in Solomons Portico. If you've never been to Jerusalem, you may not know that the Temple Mount was paved with stones, and they would have been quite clean. This is because prior to entering the Temple mount complex, one would have washed their feet, or quite possibly their entire body, in the *Mikveh* (ritual baths) located at the southern entrance to the temple mount. I present the idea that what Jesus did in John 8:6 is very similar to what the Father did in Exodus 31:18. As God wrote on the stone tablets with His finger, it is my position that in the same way, Jesus wrote into the stone ground of the Temple Mount with His finger. Could this have been a significant factor in what turned the angry mob of religious leaders away from stoning this woman? It's difficult to say for sure, but I have heard many preachers and Bible teachers speculate about the content of the message without ever considering that it may have been the finger of God incarnate writing in stone before their very eyes that sent the Pharisees packing.

Words existed before the universe, words are literally older than dirt.

Regardless, the takeaway is that God knows how to write, and when He does, it is powerful and able to be understood by His audience. The finger of God writes in human language throughout the pages of scripture, and again, this should come as no surprise since God is the author of the original language. Understand that words are not man's invention. Words existed before the universe; words are literally older than dirt.

An Original Language

Now when I say "original and divine language," there was a single, original language throughout the Earth. The words God spoke to bring Adam to life were in the same language Adam used to name all the animals. This was indeed the same language used by all people until God "confused" and broke up the language of men into many languages because of mankind's seemingly unlimited appetite to bring glory to themselves.

We see this original scenario in Genesis 11:1, which tells us, "Now the whole earth used the same language and the same words." There was no division among the people. Nothing got lost in translation. The beautiful language of God allowed all men to work together for a common purpose. They were building a tower, a Ziggurat on the Plain of Shinar. Unfortunately, humans were falling into the same sin as satan and were looking to make a "name" for themselves. This was not a city built for God's glory but for men's glory. Pride was building the city. God saw the people's pride and wicked intent to essentially be divine and decided to separate them.

Now see if you can catch the interesting part in Genesis 11:7-8, where God decides to separate the peoples and original language into multiple languages:

> ⁷'Come, let Us go down and there confuse their language, so that they will not understand one another's speech.' ⁸ So the LORD scattered them abroad from there over the face of the whole earth; and they stopped building the city.

Did you catch that? It is nuanced, but the LORD says, "let Us" go down there. What is translated in English as "the LORD" refers to a plurality of divinity. More on that later.

So "the LORD confused the language of the whole earth; and from there the LORD scattered them abroad over the face of the whole earth" (Genesis 11:9). So much discussion has been had about the mystery of the people groups of Earth. The Word of God spells it out plainly. God divided the people and spread them out over the earth. People groups from every location on Earth are all the direct descendants of Noah. Given the powerful DNA computing that is available today, check out Answers in Genesis for some fascinating research on this topic.

It would be good for us to take just a moment and look at the Hebrew language and the way it has been represented in writing for the last 6000 years. The scriptures clearly teach that before the LORD divided the nations at Babel, all men spoke the same language. When God created man, He called him Adam, which is a Hebrew name. It is a well-respected idea that Hebrew closely resembles the language of Eden. The Bible teaches that a flood destroyed the world and that the only men who lived through it were Noah, Shem, Ham, and Japheth. The biblical record shows that Shem's descendent migrated towards Canaan, Ham toward Egypt and Africa, and Japheth towards the North and East of Babylon. The Hebrew of Moses is a Semitic language.

The word Semitic can more correctly be called Shemitic as it is a language derived from the line of Shem. The Hebrew language evolved over time. The first form of written Hebrew is pictographic Hebrew, an alphabet of pictures representing concrete ideas. It brings to mind Egyptian Hieroglyphics. Pictographic Hebrew is a divine form of written communication using pictures to represent concrete items to communicate ideas. From this pictographic form of Hebrew came a phonetic script known as paleo-Hebrew. Paleo-Hebrew utilizes more abstract characters to represent sounds. The Dead Sea scrolls that were

Pictographic Hebrew is a form of written communication using pictures to communicate ideas.

found in the mid-twentieth century in Qumran, Israel, contain paleo-Hebrew elements. When Israeli academia was deported to Babylon in 586 BC, the Aramean script was adopted by the Hebrews, and the paleo-Hebrew was replaced by the more refined Semitic script of the Arameans. This is the Hebrew script that is in use today. Interestingly, the paleo-Hebrew was not abandoned by the Samaritans because they were not removed from the land.

Proto-Sinaitic Hebrew

The earliest known form of Hebrew writings is a pictographic script. The earliest Hebrew is Abraham. Abraham was called by God out of Ur. Ur is smack dab in the middle of the birthplace of humanity. Right down the street from the Plain of Shinar and occupied by people who were not dispersed elsewhere at the Tower of Babel. There are some questions worth asking at this point. What script did Abraham, Isaac, and Jacob use to communicate in writing? How did the Hebrew slaves come to use the proto-Sinaitic script as it was discovered in Sinai and dated to the eighteenth century BC? These earliest known examples of Hebrew writing are attributed to Hebrew slaves working in the mining operations of the Egyptians in Sinai.

The alphabet of this early Hebrew pictographic language is composed of pictures. Pictographic Hebrew is called proto-Sinaitic Hebrew, meaning "original" script from the Sinai region (the earliest examples date back to the eighteenth century BC). In the proto-Sinaitic script, the so-called letters represented concrete ideas. For example, the first letter, *aleph*, is represented by a bull's head. The second letter *beit* is a picture of a tent. These are concrete images that represent concrete ideas.

Consider the words of Jesus in Mark 14:36, "And He was saying, "Abba! Father! All things are possible for You; remove this cup from Me; yet not what I will, but what You will." Jesus, the Son of God, is quoting original Hebrew in His prayer to the Father. The original Hebrew is not *Abba* but rather *AB*. The Hebrew word for "father" is made up of *aleph* and *beit,* therefore, Jesus is referring to His Father as the "bull" or "strength" of the "house." So "father" in Hebrew is rooted in the idea that the father is the strength or power of the house.

Proto-Sinaitic Hebrew is the great-grandfather of our modern alphabet. Just think about the word "alphabet"—it is composed of the Hebrew *aleph* and *beit, the first two characters of the early Hebrew script.* The letter "A," in

English, is abstract; it is the phonetical representation of the sounds "ay" or "aah ." There are a few ways to say it, but no matter how you pronounce it, it is simply a character representing a sound. The *aleph* in Hebrew sounds like "A," but it carries a profound pictographic representation beyond the sound. It has the meaning of strength, power, and prominence, as well as representing the number one.

Proto-Sinaitic Hebrew is the great-grandfather of our modern alphabet.

There is a deeper meaning well beyond the sound. Don't you find it interesting that it is logical for us to connect the Aleph with God? God the Father is First, Powerful, the origin of all things, and is described in the Hebrew prayer of Shema as "one." Now, look at the various numbers of cults and false gods who have taken on the image of the bull as their symbol. This is not an accident; this is intentional. The enemy is a liar and loves to twist the realities of the universe that point to God and redirect them toward himself.

The Proto-Sinaitic Mindset

To illustrate the difference in mindset between communication in proto-Sinaitic Hebrew (early Hebrew) and modern English, consider the popular worship song Good Good Father[1] by Chris Tomlin. It's a lovely song, but what does a "good" father mean? Most of us probably picture our idea of someone who is a good father when it is our own father or another we imagine is an exemplary dad. The truth, however, is subjective and doesn't carry any real weight to it. For example, food can be good. A joke can be good. Weather can be good. Now consider another popular songwriter, King David. When speaking of God, he wrote, "The LORD is my shepherd" (Psalm 23:1). A shepherd is not just "good." The shepherd cares for his sheep, protects them, and loves them. He will even lay down his life to defend and rescue them. Now that is a powerful image with some serious weight. In Psalm 18:2, David also says, "The Lord is my rock and my fortress and my deliverer, My God, my rock, in whom I take refuge; My shield and the horn of my salvation, my stronghold." In the pages of the Bible, we encounter eastern men who think in concrete, eastern ways. We westerners tend to think in terms of the abstract. Our words have definitions, but they lack the concrete imagery of the eastern mind. Chris Tomlin says that God is a "Good Good Father"; this is true in the abstract western mind. King David says that God is a "Shepherd," a "Rock," and a "Strong Tower." These are also true but are concrete images with a strong eastern perspective. This is the difference in thinking between the abstract western mind and the concrete eastern mind.

From this, we begin to understand that scripture was written to express concrete, not abstract, ideas. The Old Testament was written predominantly in Hebrew by Hebrews. The New Testament was written primarily in Greek, but still, most of the authors were Hebrews. In our current time, we English-speaking Americans are in great danger of missing the point when translating the scriptures. While God's Word was written under the guidance of His Holy Spirit by eastern thinkers, it is read and interpreted in English by western thinkers. As a result, there is an inevitable disconnect. Some Hebrew concepts will be completely lost on English speakers. Please understand that if you are going to experience the profound revelation unveiled in this book, you must grasp the concept that God's name is rooted in concrete ideas.

I'll give you an example. As I've mentioned, the second letter of the proto-Sinaitic Hebrew alphabet is *beit*. As stated earlier, this translates as "tent," but we can also translate it as "house" (tents being the homes of most of the writers of the Old Testament). You can pronounce it as *beit, bet*, or *beth*. In Israel, they pronounce Bethlehem as *Bet-le-hem*. It means "the house of bread" (*hem* translates as bread). Now think about John 6:35, where Jesus says, "I am the bread of life . . . ," and He was born in the "Town of Bread." You'll never get that from simply reading the word in English.

Intimations like this were not lost on the apostle Paul when he wrote his letters that would come to make up the bulk of the New Testament. For example, in Romans 8:15, Paul writes, "For you have not received a spirit of slavery leading to fear again, but you have received a spirit of adoption as sons by which we cry out, 'Abba! Father!'" As we saw earlier, in Hebrew, the word for father is *AB*. In proto-Sinaitic Hebrew, the father is the strength or the power of the home. Paul is accentuating your born-again adopted status by quoting the Hebrew for "Father."

There are some essential realities we must take away. First, God called Abraham out of Ur and created the Hebrew nation as the canvas on which to write His gospel story. Abraham was called from the center of creation, where the garden's original language and writing remained. Proto-Sinaitic Hebrew is the earliest form of Hebrew of which we are aware. It was written pictographically, and the earliest findings of this writing style date back to the eighteenth century BC.

Curse Amulet

While I was writing this book in the spring of 2022, a significant discovery in biblical archeology was revealed. At the foot of Mount Ebal in Israel, archeologists unearthed a lead curse amulet (a lead notebook with writing carved in the lead). Analysis of the lead placed its origin back to the fourteenth century BC, right around the time of Israel's exodus from Egypt. Remember, in the time of Joshua, Mount Gerizim was the mount of blessing, while Mount Ebal was the mount of cursing. "It shall come about, when the LORD your God brings you into the land where you are entering to possess it, that you shall place the blessing on Mount Gerizim and the curse on Mount Ebal" (Deuteronomy 11:29).

The lead curse amulet was folded in half, so it was only possible to tell what was written on the inside once the archaeologists took it to Prague. There they did a tomographic scan of it and found a clear Hebrew curse inside. Within this curse, written in proto-Sinaitic (pictographic) Hebrew, was the name of God. This discovery provides powerful evidence that pictographic Hebrew was the writing form in the fourteenth century BC when Moses led the Israelite exodus from Egypt. The writing found inside the amulet displays a sophisticated writing style and script that can convey clear messages in the written word. This writing style would have been in use when God revealed His name to Moses. I believe it is the most significant archeological finding since the discovery of the Dead Sea scrolls.

What three things do most major people groups on earth seem to have in common? A flood narrative, pyramids, and an early pictographic writing style. First, a flood narrative is common among ancient people groups across the globe. This makes sense because their ancestors were all descendants of those who rode out the flood in the ark. The story would have been handed down through many generations and in many different languages, but the crux would have remained the same. Remember, the LORD confused the language of all the people; He did not wipe their memories. Some details would likely change as the new languages would struggle to have other words to describe the events. Much like the telephone game played at children's parties, the story would morph over time and across cultures, but the root is common.

Secondly, many ancient people groups also built pyramids (or ziggurats). Travel to Africa, and you find pyramids. Travel to South and Central America, and you find pyramids. Travel to the Orient, and you find pyramids. When the LORD dispersed the people (whatever that looked like, I can hardly imagine), they would have begun with similar skill sets and ideas from a shared background. In fact, some believe the Tower of Babel was envisioned as a giant ziggurat. With different words to describe the building process, it's only natural that the end designs diverged, resulting in different architectures among different people groups. However, there are striking similarities across the globe in pyramid design details and the era of construction.

The third and most pertinent similarity across most ancient people groups is *pictographic* writing. Not cave paintings made by ignorant Cro-Magnon men, but pictographic communications using word pictures representing concrete concepts to document language. Again, this makes sense because all language was originally the same with the same written form. As the dispersed people groups began speaking their new languages and needed to communicate in writing what was being said, it only follows that they would try to write in the manner they always had—drawing pictures to represent the ideas they wanted to convey. This is important to understand as we follow Israel's birth as a nation and how God reveals Himself to them throughout the generations.

A Brief Biblical History

Let's follow the biblical record because it is vital to understand the path of the Hebrew written language and why this becomes so amazingly important in the story of God and His creation. The LORD separates the nations, then calls Abram out of Ur of the Chaldees. Abram obeys, God changes his name to Abraham, and Abraham begets Isaac. Isaac begets Jacob. Jacob has four wives and thirteen children—twelve sons and a daughter named Dinah. The nation of Israel is born. Jacob's favorite son is Joseph, who has prophetic dreams that cause his brothers to hate him further. They sell Joseph off to slave traders, who sell him to the Egyptians. God uses Joseph to provide a safe haven for the family of Jacob (Israel), and due to a severe famine and lack of food, all of the Israelites end up in Egypt. After a few generations, they are enslaved, and Moses is born.

Moses is a fascinating guy. The Pharaoh gives the order to kill all the young Hebrew males because he's afraid they're getting too powerful. God is obviously blessing them. Moses' mom puts him in a basket covered in pitch (just like the ark!) in the river, full of crocodiles and danger. Pharaoh's daughter hears baby Moses' cries in the reeds, and she adopts him and hires who else but Moses' mom to be a wet nurse? So the very child the Pharaoh was trying to kill ends up being raised in his household with all its privileges.

The New Testament gives us some fascinating insight into the royal life of Moses. Acts 7:22 says, "Moses was educated in all the learning of the Egyptians, and he was a man of power in words and deeds." This is a New Testament writer. Moses was educated in *all* the learning of the Egyptians, and he was a man of power in words and deeds. In fact, the historical record (Josephus) states that Moses served as a mighty Egyptian general in the Ethiopian campaign before the age of forty.

Jump to Acts 7:23-29. Here it is noted that Moses is forty years old. He goes out to see his Hebrew brethren, tries to save them in his own strength, and kills an Egyptian slavedriver. Pharaoh is furious and gives the order to find and execute him for killing an Egyptian over an Israelite slave. So Moses flees to Midian, just across the Gulf of Aqaba from Sinai. Now pay close attention. Midian is very close to Sinai and where we find Mount Horeb (some believe that

Horeb/Sinai are on the Saudi Arabian side of the Gulf of Aqaba). After forty years, this is where Moses has a history-changing interaction with the LORD in the burning bush. "When the LORD saw that he turned aside to look, God called to him from the midst of the bush and said, 'Moses, Moses!' And he said, 'Here I am'" (Exodus 3:4).

Bear in mind Moses has been trained in the language and the words of Egypt. Now Moses, with all his education and literacy, is on the back side of the Sinai desert in Midian. During this time, Egypt controls most of the Sinai, and Midian is just across the Gulf of Aqaba. Moses puts a little space between himself and Pharaoh. So we've established the fact that God speaks, and God writes. Moses then, by the divine hand of God, gets placed in the finest schools in Egypt. He writes and reads in Egyptian for forty years until his killing of the Egyptian slave master. Then he spends forty years in Midian, marrying Jethro's daughter and living amongst Jethro's family and people. It is not unreasonable to think that after forty years in Midian, Moses would have learned and adopted their language and writing style. Some of the first proto-Sinaitic Hebrew inscriptions date back to the eighteenth century BC and have been attributed to Hebrew slaves assigned to Egyptian mining operations in Sinai during this period. These connections are important, so bear with me.

Fast forward to Exodus 17:14, and something interesting happens here: "Then the LORD said to Moses, 'Write this in a book as a memorial and recite it to Joshua, that I will utterly blot out the memory of Amalek from under heaven.'" It is widely accepted that Moses is the author of the Torah—Genesis, Exodus, Leviticus, Numbers, and Deuteronomy, which appears to be a direct result of the LORD commanding Moses to record everything for Joshua and posterity. Many scholars have taken the position that the Hebrew language was not refined enough for Moses to have written it in this time frame. That is not what the Bible says, however. The Bible says that God commanded Moses to write it, and that he had the skills and that he wrote it.

God is just!—He wouldn't tell Moses to write things down if Moses wasn't capable of writing things down. The scriptures have already described that Moses was powerful in words. So what exactly did it look like? What script did Moses use to communicate the messages and the Law of God? What Moses encountered in Midian and likely learned from the Israelites in Egypt was likely proto-Sinaitic or pictographic Hebrew. There are several reasons I believe this. For the sake of brevity, however, I'm going to simply state the case that Abraham was from Ur of the Chaldees (the original neighborhood of the Tower of Babel), later to become ancient Babylon, in what is now modern-day Iraq. The original Semitic Hebrew language was very close to the language God spoke to Adam and Eve in the garden and what God spoke to Noah pre and post-flood. The people left in the plain of Shinar (Iraq) were the people God chose to leave there during the separation of men, as described in Genesis 11.

Now, let's go back to Moses. He obeys God and heads to Egypt to confront Pharaoh. There is a period of time where the heart of Pharaoh is hardened, and the power of God is displayed in a series of plagues that are visited on the people of Egypt. In the last of these plagues, we find the

Hebrews sacrificing a lamb and covering their doorposts with the blood. During the night, an angel of death visits Egypt, and the firstborn son of every Egyptian family dies. It is this plague which breaks the will of Pharaoh and the Egyptian people. The Hebrews are sent away with goods (gifts the Egyptians gave them). Moses leads the nation of Israel to the Red Sea, where they end up between an ocean and Pharaoh, who is angry and has changed his mind regarding the freedom of the Hebrew slaves. God parts the waters, and the nation of Israel is saved. The army of Egypt attempts to follow and is swallowed up by the same waters. Now we find ourselves with the Israelites sometime after the Exodus from Egypt, after they have crossed the Red Sea. They are camped at the foot of Mount Sinai, or what is also referred to as Mount Horeb. This mountain where they are camped just happens to be the same mountain where the LORD revealed Himself to Moses in the burning bush. So now we have Moses up on this mountain with the LORD, spending time and learning the Law of God (God is explaining who He is to Moses and what the parameters of their relationship will be). The people can hear the voice of the LORD, and they see the fire and smoke and are terrified. During this time period, the LORD writes for Moses a copy of the Law on stone tablets with His very finger.

The question that I leave you with is this: If you had your very own Indiana Jones moment and were able to pry open the Ark of the Covenant and have a peek at the very handwriting of God, what would it look like? In the next chapter, we'll begin to reveal more answers to this mystery and continue to lay some groundwork for why the answer to this question has powerful implications for living a transformed, Spirit-filled, born-again life today, some 3,500 years later.

A Word Changes Everything

God chose to reveal His true name to Moses about 3,500 years ago. As He spoke His name, the LORD added a little history lesson for Moses. Exodus 6:2-3 says, "God spoke further to Moses and said to him, 'I am the LORD; and I appeared to Abraham, Isaac, and Jacob, as God Almighty, but by My name, LORD [YHVH], I did not make Myself known to them.'" The phrase "God Almighty" in the passage above is translated from the Hebrew *El Shaddai.*

What God was telling Moses is that He had not revealed Himself to Abraham, Isaac, and Jacob in the same way He was revealing Himself now to Moses. The Patriarchs of old did not know the true name of God. They worshipped Him without knowing the true name, using the generic name for deity, as I will explain shortly. Now the name of God was at last known to man. The proper name of God is *YHVH*, which translates as "I am" or "Existent One." Imagine the awe Moses must have felt as the first to hear God speak His name.

The name of God is a powerful word. Jesus uses similar wording in the New Testament in John 8:58, when He states, "Before Abraham was born, I <u>am</u>." Critics like to say Jesus never claimed to be God, but that is simply untrue. When Jesus calls Himself, "I am," He is proclaiming that He is God. In Exodus 6:2, God is telling Moses that Abraham, Isaac, and Jacob simply knew Him as *El Shaddai* or God Almighty. They did not know His true name. In Hebrew, *El* is a generic reference to the idea of deity. *Elohim* is a reference to deity in the *plural*.

The name God reveals to Moses is a new revelation; it is entirely different. The name *YHVH* is powerful, prophetic, and profound. Whenever you see names in scripture ending in "yah" or "jah," it references the proper name of God. For example, the word "hallelujah" is a Hebrew word meaning <u>all praise to *YHVH*</u>. Names like Jehovah Jireh (provider) and Jehovah Rapha (healer) are descriptions of Jehovah. Jehovah is simply one of the ways people say YHVH in English.

Elohim Is Not God's Name

The Word of God opens in Genesis 1:1 with the phrase, "In the beginning, God *[Elohim]* created the heavens and the earth." By the fourth verse of Chapter 2 of Genesis, Moses switches to YHVH. Genesis 2:4 says, "This is the account of the heavens and the earth when they were created, in the day that the LORD God [YHVH] made earth and heaven." From Genesis 1:1 through Genesis 2:3, Moses used the word *Elohim* to describe God, but in Genesis 2:4, he switches to calling God by His revealed name YHVH. This is a subtle but essential transition you won't catch if you aren't looking at the original language.

I would not die on this hill, but I propose the fall of satan and the angels occurs during this time. At the beginning of the word of God, the idea of false gods is off the table, and by the fourth verse of Chapter 2, it is a reality. It's important to understand that *Elohim* is not God's name. *Elohim* is the idea or concept of deity, not the proper name of God. In Exodus 20:3, God says, "You shall have no other gods [*elohims*] before Me." Here in the Ten Commandments, God uses the word *elohim* to refer to false gods. When YHVH describes the pagan gods of Egypt, he uses the word *elohim*. When referring to Himself in Malachi 3:6, He says, "For I, the LORD [YHVH], do not change; therefore you, O sons of Jacob, are not consumed." Here, God uses His actual name, not a description of who He is.

The bottom line is that the proper name of God is YHVH, not *Elohim!*

The mystery, however, goes even deeper. As alluded to earlier, the Hebrew word *Elohim* is a plural noun. Therefore, when God is described as *Elohim*, He is undeniably being described as a plural God. In this way, we see the revelation of the Trinity all the way back to the first verse in the Bible. We'll dive into this in greater depth later in the book. For now, recognize that Moses, the man who spent significant amounts of time in God's presence, makes the very specific point of describing God with the Hebrew plural noun *Elohim*. Just as he experienced the plural nature of God, he wanted to be certain future generations did not miss it.

Moving forward to the passage of Exodus 12:12, specifically to the final plague God brought against the Egyptian people, we read, "For I will go through the land of Egypt on that night, and will strike down all the firstborn in the land of Egypt, both man and beast; and against all the gods *[elohim's]* of Egypt I will execute judgments—I am the LORD [YHVH]." As we can see, the *elohim's* of Egypt are not YHVH. They are false gods, imposters of the one true God. The *elohim's* of Egypt were delusional men, demons—spiritual forces of wickedness in heavenly places. They were anything but YHVH.

The bottom line is that the proper name of God is YHVH, not Elohim!

Why Do English Translations Choose the Word LORD?

When we read Genesis 2:4, we observe that the Hebrew word YHVH was translated into English as "LORD." Why did the translators choose this word and then put it in all capitals? In English, "Lord" is not a proper noun, so why would it be capitalized here? To understand this, you must know that during the intertestamental period (the time between Malachi and Matthew), the Old Testament was translated into Greek. A group of seventy Hebrew sages made that initial translation, which for that reason came to be called the Septuagint (seventy). The sages used the word "*Theos*" for YHVH in the Genesis 2:4 passage and the word "*Kyrios*" for the Exodus 6:3 passage. The English word Lord is a close translation for the Greek word *Kyrios*. Likely due to Jewish tradition, they did not want to write the name YHVH out of reverence.

In the context of the twenty-first century, I see this as a terrible mistake. Let me offer you a few words to show why I see this as a grave mistake: Lord Vader, Lord of the Rings, Lord Grantham, good lord, and oh my lord. In twenty-first-century western culture, the word "lord" is not a proper noun. It certainly doesn't hold any of the reverence that should be ascribed to the singular, divine, and unspeakable name of the Creator of all things. Lord, as it is used in the Septuagint and then subsequently in the New Testament, simply means "the one to whom a thing belongs, or master."

A Word about the Name of God

Out of deep reverence, the ancient Hebrew sages did not like to write or say the name of God aloud. Just before the birth of Christ, the Essene scribes of Qumran would bathe, or *mikveh*, both before and after writing the unspeakable name of God. To this very day, our Jewish brothers avoid writing or speaking the name of God. When they write it, they omit the vowels, like this: G_D. This is because they do not want to risk breaking the commandment by carelessly using the Name of God.

When referencing the name of God today, Jewish people often use the word _Hashem_. *Hashem* is the Hebrew word meaning "The name." The phonetical pronunciation of the word is *Ha shame*, which is fascinating because, in twenty-first-century English, shame is anything but a reference to the unspeakable name of God. To this day, Jewish rabbis use the word *Hashem* when referring to God.

Another alternate word for the divine name used by the Jews is *Adonai*, which means "my Lord" or "Lord" in Hebrew. It comes from the Hebrew root "*adon*," which means firm, strong, Lord, Master. *Adonai* and *Hashem* are used to say the name of God without saying the name of God. There is a deep beauty in such reverence that is lost on most English-speaking people and is undoubtedly lost in the English translation of God's Word. While God revealed His name to Moses in Hebrew, we are reading it in English today.

We must remember when we read capital L-O-R-D in the English Old Testament, we are not reading the name of God as He revealed it to Moses. We are reading an English word that was used to correlate to the Greek word *Kyrios*. This word was used by the seventy sages in the original translation of the Old Testament from Hebrew to Greek. LORD is not the proper name of God; YHVH is.

The Tetragrammaton

As revealed to Moses, the proper name of God is YHVH. This is a proper noun. In Hebrew, the word YHVH has four characters. This four-character name of God is referred to as the Tetragrammaton. Tetragrammaton is a Greek word meaning to have four characters. This Tetragrammaton represents the proper name of God. Since it is God's proper name, this is obviously a huge deal! The four Hebrew characters in God's proper name are *YOD, HEY, VAV,* and *HEY.* As I previously mentioned, there are no vowels in the proto-Sinaitic pictographic Hebrew script. Since there are no vowels, no one knows for sure how the *YOD, HEY, VAV,* and *HEY* that form the unspeakable name of God are pronounced in the ancient Hebrew language. For this book, we have chosen the translation of YHVH because of the *Vav (which can also be translated as WAW).*

Tetragrammaton is a Greek word meaning to have four characters.

Some translate the Tetragrammaton as *Yahveh,* and some as *Yahweh.* Others translate it as *Jehovah.*

Understand that no matter which form of the word is used in translation, it is always a reference to the Hebrew word for the unspeakable name of God: the Tetragrammaton YHVH. Again, since there are no vowels in proto-Sinaitic pictographic Hebrew, nobody knows the exact pronunciation.

None of the Bible Was Written in English

While we do not know the true pronunciation of God's name, Moses did. He heard God speak it to him, and he saw God write it on stone tablets. Unfortunately, since proto-Sinaitic pictographic Hebrew does not include vowels, Moses recorded the name he heard God speak without vowels. It is important to note that none of the Bible was written in English. Most of it was written in Hebrew and Greek. Be careful to remember this. Use modern web tools like www.blueletterbible.com to provide insight and clarity on the original languages. Praise God that we live in a day where such tools are free and readily available for our study.

The Bible was written first in proto-Sinaitic pictographic Hebrew, then translated into paleo-Hebrew, and then into modern Aramaic Hebrew. Even within the Hebrew language itself, there is a translational legacy. As with all transitions, we lose some nuances in translation. In the last chapter, we talked about the pictographic Hebrew and how it is rooted in God's original language and writing. From there, the language moved to phonetically based characters to represent the sounds in paleo-Hebrew, and eventually it morphed into a more modern Aramaic script.

It is important to note that none of the Bible was written in English.

As we dig deeper throughout this book, we will see the proto-Sinaitic pictographic Hebrew name of God woven throughout the entire Bible. We will unveil these realities in the chapters to come, and you will see the unspeakable name of God and the references to the proto-Sinaitic pictographic Hebrew version of His name in almost all of scripture. This was God's plan.

A Singular Name for a Plural God

The writings of Moses clearly established this plurality through his choice of words, which is affirmed by the New Testament. In Matthew 28:19, Jesus was crystal-clear that God is plural, "Go therefore and make disciples of all the nations, baptizing them in the name of the Father and the Son and the Holy Spirit." When Jesus said, ". . . baptizing them in the name . . ." the Greek word used here is *Onema*, or "the Name." It refers to a singular name, meaning there is a *singular name* for the Father, Son, and Holy Spirit. *That name is YHVH.* The Name, the Tetragrammaton, is a name that is above every name.

The Name above Every Name

An important question that was emerging from my research was, "Why would a triune God reveal Himself in a *four-character name?*" I also had to wonder why we used a regular, plain, and ordinary noun when we translated such a magnificent name into English. To call YHVH "LORD" in English is a terrible affront. It lacks the majesty, reverence, awe, and, more importantly, the deep *meaning* represented by the proper name of God as it was originally given.

There is a mystery here. Something is unfolding with regard to the name of YHVH. The seventy sages of the Septuagint replaced the glorious proper noun name of God YHVH with a common word *Kyrios*. The English translators followed suit by using the word LORD to represent the name of God. Consequently, the original pictographic font of Moses has been lost to the phonetical fonts of later cultures, and the deep meaning of God's name has become obscured by time and culture. In the next chapter, we will unveil how the proto-Sinaitic pictographic Hebrew name of God, YHVH, which we represent in English with the uppercase LORD, shows up in the New Testament in a powerful and exciting new way. That is where we are going next.

The Name of *Jesus*

The word LORD YHVH, translated into English, occurs 6,521 times from Genesis to Malachi. In Malachi 4:5, the prophet writes, "Behold, I am going to send you Elijah the prophet before the coming of the great and terrible day of the LORD." This is the last usage of the word LORD, YHVH, in the scriptures. As we flip the pages from Malachi to Matthew, the word LORD YHVH is gone! The proper name of God in Hebrew is completely missing from the New Testament, or is it? The word "Lord" (*kyrios*) appears 717 times in the New Testament. As mentioned in the previous chapter, the word from which they translate it is the Greek word *kyrios*[2]. To the casual observer, the word LORD in the Old Testament is now just Lord in the New Testament; however, they are two very different words with two very different meanings.

The first time we encounter the word "Lord" in the New Testament is in Matthew 1:20. There's very little physical space between the last usage in the Old Testament and the first usage in the New Testament of the word "Lord." Still, the difference between the two words is enormous.

> [20] But when he had considered this, behold, an angel of the <u>Lord</u> appeared to him in a dream, saying, "Joseph, son of David, do not be afraid to take Mary as your wife; for the Child who has been conceived in her is of the Holy Spirit."

Looking at the Greek, "an angel of the Lord" is translated from an angel of *Kyrios*. What happened to LORD YHVH? How does the proper, revealed name of God disappear completely from scripture after 6,521 distinct name drops in the Old Testament? What is going on here? Let's take a closer look.

From Genesis to Malachi

The translators of the Old Testament used the English word LORD when translating the unspeakable name of God. YHVH is a proper noun roughly translated as the "I AM" or the "Existing One." Remember how this whole thing started for me with the phrase "YHVH *Elohim*," which translates as "The God who really is"?

Would you agree that this is a profoundly simple name for an indescribable God? YHVH (YOD, HEY, VAV, HEY) is only four characters wide, but it is a million miles deep. Malachi 3:6 says, "For I, the <u>LORD</u>, do not change; therefore you, O sons of Jacob, are not consumed." Hebrews 13:8 is a New Testament parallel to Malachi 3:6. It says, "Jesus

Christ *is* the same yesterday and today and forever." There is a strikingly similar message in those two passages.

Think about this for a second . . . what we know is that God does not change. We know God has a proper noun name. We also know that the proper noun name of YVHV disappears in the New Testament, so something is going on here. Like all cases of disappearing persons, a mystery must be solved. We are going to investigate this mystery.

From Matthew to Revelation

From Matthew to Revelation, the word "Lord" (*Kyrios*) means something entirely different from the word "LORD" YHVH we see from Genesis to Malachi. In the New Testament, the word "Lord" is translated from the Greek *Kyrios*. *Kyrios* is an ordinary masculine noun. Roughly translated as *"he to whom a person or thing belongs, about which he has power of deciding; master, lord[3]"*. While the definition of *Kyrios* or (Lord) certainly does describe God, *Kyrios* is not a proper name. There is nothing inherently divine or majestic about it. *Kyrios* is not YHVH! To muddy the waters even further, the translators of the Septuagint also chose to translate *YHVH* as *Kyrios*. As we touched on earlier, there may have been an honorable reason for this; however, it certainly creates some confusion.

How Long Have You Been a Christian?

Okay, so we have defined the mystery. Why is the proper name of God, LORD YHVH, missing from the New Testament? I want to ask you a question. It's a simple question, so hang in there with me. "What does the name of

Jesus mean?" Having asked this of many born-again people over the years, it's fascinating how so many have no idea what the name of Jesus means, nor from where it came. Many of us, including myself, have prayed to Jesus for decades without the faintest idea of what His name means. We have asked for help and salvation, mercy and power, and never stopped to ask the simple question: What does the name of Jesus mean, and from where does it come?

A New Name Declared?

In the narrative of Matthew 1:18-21, an angel of the Lord comes to Joseph in a dream. Joseph was already dealing with the fact the woman he was supposed to marry was pregnant. This reality was no small piece of drama in first century Judaism, as becoming pregnant out of wedlock could have profound consequences for the rest of your life. Having an angel appear to him at night must have added to his anxiety. As Joseph was about to discover, however, the angel had come to "simmer him down," as my dad often says.

> [18] Now the birth of Jesus Christ was as follows: when His mother Mary had been betrothed to Joseph, before they came together she was found to be with child by the Holy Spirit. [19] And Joseph her husband, being a righteous man and not wanting to disgrace her, planned to send her away secretly. [20] But when he had considered this, behold, an angel of the Lord appeared to him in a dream, saying, "Joseph, son of David, do not be afraid to take Mary as your wife; for the Child who has been conceived in her is of the Holy Spirit. [21] She will bear a Son; and you shall call His name Jesus, for He will save His people from their sins."

Now that they had been visited by an angel of God, Mary and Joseph knew a few things for sure: the baby was not the result of any sexual union but was the divine power of the Holy Spirit in the life and body of Mary that had caused her to become pregnant. Therefore, Joseph knew he could confidently take this young lady as his wife without fear or doubt of her fidelity. As a side note, I have always wondered if there was no room at the inn for Mary because of her "unplanned pregnancy." I'm sure it was a tough sell to convince the extended family (who were all gathered in Bethlehem) that you were the first person in the history of the universe to become pregnant without a man.

Another thing they knew for certain was what they were to name the baby. The child's name would be *Jesus*, which is immensely significant. I am about to show you that the name of Jesus is a divine name. In the same way the triune God declared His name, YHVH, to

The child's name would be Jesus.

Moses, the Father declares the name of His Son, Jesus, to Joseph and Mary. The jaw-dropping part is that the name God revealed to Moses, YHVH, some 3,500 years earlier, *would be baked into the name of His Son*. There would be no debate. The child's name was not up for discussion.

Jesus Is an English Word

It's worth recognizing that "Jesus" is an English word. In what language did the angel reveal the name of Jesus to Joseph and Mary? Hebrew? Greek? Aramaic? I wish I could tell you, be we don't know. What I can say with relative certainty, seeing as how the English language would not come onto the world stage for about another 600 years, is that the angel did not speak the name of Jesus in English. As westerners, it's good for us to remember that Hebrew people, who predominantly wrote the Bible, used the Hebrew and Greek languages. Taking the time to look closely at the original languages bears much fruit when digging into the Bible.

A Word about Transliteration

Before going further, we need to pause briefly and discuss something technical. Specifically, I need you to understand the difference between translation and transliteration. Transliteration is "the act, process, or result of writing letters or words using the corresponding characters of another alphabet or writing system"[4]. So a transliteration is simply a word that looks like a word in another language. On the other hand, translation is "the rendering of something into another language." For instance, agua is Spanish for water. These two words are accurately translated back and forth between languages, and they don't look or sound anything like each other.

Armed with your newly acquired knowledge of transliteration, let me show you something fascinating. The English word "Jesus" is a transliteration of the Greek word *Iēsous*[5]. *Iēsous* is a transliteration of the Hebrew word *Yᵊhôšûa*[6], otherwise spelled *Yehoshua*, or Joshua. Now check this out: in Hebrew, Joshua (*Yᵊhôšûa*) is the combination of two Hebrew words: *YHVH* and *Yasa*, meaning "YHVH is salvation." So, follow me here; the transliteration goes from Yᵊhôšûa ˋ to *Iēsous* to Jesus. Tracing the transliteration back, we see the English word Jesus derives directly from the Hebrew YHVH, the unspeakable name of God.

So the Tetragrammaton YHVH does not disappear in the New Testament after all.

Matthew 1:21 says, "She will bear a Son; and you shall call His name <u>Jesus</u>, for He will <u>save</u> His people from their sins." This is astounding! The angel of the Lord told Mary to call the child Jesus (YHVH is Salvation) because He would save His people from their sins. Jesus is not a new name coming on the scene here in the New Testament. It is none other than YHVH

The English word Jesus derives directly from the Hebrew YHVH.

showing up in the New Testament with a glorified name! Hallelujah (All Praise to YHVH)!

Following the transliteration backward, we can clearly see that YHVH is predominant in the name of Jesus (or *Yehoshua*). When I recognized this, it blew my mind! Here we are again with the unspeakable name of God, but the incarnate Christ (Messiah, which is Hebrew for "anointed one") amplifies it. Matthew 1:23 says, "Behold, the virgin shall be with child and shall bear a Son, and they shall call His name 'Immanuel,' which translated means, 'God with us.'" This is a direct callback to Isaiah 7:14: "Therefore the Lord Himself will give you a sign: Behold, a virgin will be with child and bear a son, and she will call His name Immanuel."

Through the miraculous virgin birth, YHVH had come to live among the people.

The Salvation of YHVH

The name of Jesus is entirely profound and supremely powerful. It is truly the name above all names. Have a look at what Paul wrote to the church in Philippians 2:9-11.

> [9] For this reason also, God [*Theos*, a reference to the Father] highly exalted Him [Jesus, the Son], and bestowed on Him [Jesus the Son] the name which is above every name [YHVH plus Salvation], [10] so that at the name of Jesus [The Salvation of YHVH] every knee will bow, of those who are in heaven and on earth and under the earth, [11] and that every tongue will confess that Jesus Christ is Lord [*Kyrios*], to the glory of God [*Theos*] the Father.

Jesus is the all-powerful name. There is no name like it. Of the name of Jesus, Luke writes in Acts 4:12, "And there is <u>salvation</u> in no one else; for there is no other name under heaven that has been given among men by which we must be saved." Only the name of Jesus can restore men to peace (shalom) with the Father and provide a covering from the penalty of their sins. There is no other way!

An Unveiling

There is an unveiling happening here. God has a proper noun name, a real and actual name. His name is YHVH, which means I AM, or "The Existing One." Remember what was happening in Egypt when God first revealed His name to Moses? There were many *elohims (false gods)* in Egypt, but there is only one YHVH. Moses met with YHVH in person, just as a man meets with another man. Also, remember that YHVH is repeatedly affirmed as plural by Moses' use of the word *Elohim*.

We then see YHVH becoming flesh in John 1:14, and YHVH in the flesh is given the name Jesus in the birth narrative of Matthew. He is named Jesus (or Joshua), meaning the "YHVH is Salvation." During His time on Earth, Jesus made clear and forthright claims to be God YHVH—I AM. In John 8:58, He said, "Before Abraham was born, I <u>am</u>." The corrupt religious leaders tried to kill Him for making such a claim. There can be no mistake or question about it—in the passages we've examined, we see Jesus unveiling Himself as the second Person of YHVH.

As we continue to unveil this 3,500-year-old mystery, the next logical question is, "How does this all fit in with the Trinity?" Well, we've discussed that the plurality of *Elohim was continually reinforced by Moses* and how the name YHVH is integrated into the incarnation of Jesus. Still, the Trinity remains the most mysterious doctrine in all of Christianity; yet it feels like the mystery of the Tetragrammaton, the four-character representation of the triune God, holds the key to understanding it all. With every discovery of the unspeakable name of YHVH, it seems we are getting closer to understanding something hidden for centuries, closer to unveiling the deeper mystery of God's name. We're on the cusp of something huge, something dramatic and unknown until now. Let's keep digging.

The Trinity

Did you know that the word "Trinity" cannot be found in either the Old or the New Testament? It might surprise you that the word Trinity did not even show up in church writings until the second-century AD. Perhaps even more astonishing is that despite the word for Trinity not existing at the time, the second word in the Bible declares the plurality of God: "In the beginning, *Elohim*" ("In the beginning" is one word in Hebrew). I have already shared with you that *Elohim* is the concept of God, and it is a masculine plural noun.

People have been discussing and debating the idea of the Trinity for almost two thousand years. It is a concept with literally nothing in the universe to compare it to, and impossible to "nail down" to a concrete definition. Dr. Steve Brown says, *"You cannot discuss the Trinity for more than thirty seconds without committing heresy."* This is funny because it is true. Explaining the mystery of God's triune nature in human terms is a near-impossible endeavor.

I grew up in the church. My testimony matches Paul's closer than Peter's. I was listening to arguments about the Trinity while I was still riding my Big Wheel. The trite evangelical answer is that the Trinity consists of three co-equal, co-eternal Persons. There are many false teachings related to the idea of the Trinity. Our Jewish brothers think we are polytheists (that we believe in multiple Gods) because of our definition. For simplicity's sake and to avoid fisticuffs, let's just agree that based on the words of Jesus Himself, the Trinity consists of the Father, the Son, and the Holy Spirit.

The word "Trinity" cannot be found in either the Old or the New Testament.

Did you know that 3,500 years ago, God drew a picture of the Trinity for Moses that was so simple even a small child could understand it? With what we've covered so far, you shouldn't be surprised that, yes, it is indeed His name, YHVH, in proto-Sinaitic pictographic Hebrew. So here's the first step in the big reveal. The following is what that picture of the unspeakable name of God looks like in proto-Sinaitic pictographic Hebrew:

For now, just study the picture and see if anything jumps out at you. Please note that Hebrew is read from right to left, so the YOD is the character on the far right, followed in sequence by the HEY, VAV, and HEY. If this is the first time you are seeing this picture in the context of Bible study, welcome home! I promise I will explain every fascinating aspect in detail, but for now, let's get back to the Trinity. As I said previously, modern evangelicals define the Trinity as three co-equal, co-eternal Persons of the Godhead. I've been a Christian my whole life and have never found this definition super helpful. Try using it on a five-year-old!

You'll often hear people describe the Trinity in terms of water. While most people's use of this metaphor is likely innocent, this is, in fact, a heresy known as modalism. Modalism is the idea that God exists in three different modes—Father, Son, and Holy Spirit—like water has three different forms: solid, liquid, and gas. The problem with modalism is it distorts and even denies the triune character of God. God is three in one, not three different *forms* of one. Remember, Jesus said in John 10:30, "I and the Father are one." He did not say, "I and the Father are two different forms of the same thing."

3,500 years ago, God drew a picture of the Trinity that was so simple even a small child could understand it.

So yes, the Trinity is extremely difficult to understand. It matches the loving nature of God that the Trinity was described and diagrammed in a divinely brilliant yet profoundly simple way. Using the picture God drew for Him as his basis, Moses regularly described the plurality of God with confidence and under inspiration.

Moses and the Plurality of God

Moses repeatedly declares the plurality of God in the Old Testament. From the very beginning of Genesis 1:26-27, he made sure we understood there was a mystery in the plural nature of God:

> [26] Then God said, "Let Us make man in Our image, according to Our likeness; and let them rule over the fish of the sea and over the birds of the sky and over the cattle and over all the earth, and over every creeping thing that creeps on the earth." [27] God created man in His own image, in the image of God He created him; male and female He created them.

When considering the concept of the Trinity, it is important to remember that Moses hung out with God. Moses was alone with God on top of the mountain for many days. He ate with God, talked with God, and when Moses came down from the mountain, he had spent so much time with God that his face shone like the sun. Moses spent time basking in the presence of God, and he came away with a very clear unders-tanding of the plurality of God. Thus, he understood the Trinity in ways the rest of us can only imagine; but it wasn't just Moses who spoke about the plurality of God.

Just as Moses did in the Old Testament, Jesus repeatedly declares the plurality of God in the New Testament.

Jesus referenced the Trinity many times. Just as Moses did in the Old Testament, Jesus repeatedly declares the plurality of God in the New Testament. In Matthew 28:19, Jesus said, "Go therefore and make disciples of all the nations, baptizing them in the name of the Father and the Son and the Holy Spirit." There is a name that represents the Father, the Son, and the Holy Spirit. It is one name, not three names, and that name, as we know, is YHVH. God drew it in picture form for Moses 3,500 years ago, and we see it today thoroughly woven throughout scripture.

Snapshots of the Father

Let's take a few moments and look at a few of these scriptural snapshots validating the Father. There are hundreds of verses in scripture describing the Father, but note that there are no verses describing anyone *sending* the Father. The Father sent Jesus. No one sent the Father. He is I Am. He always was, He is, and He forever will be. He inhabits eternity (Isaiah 57:15).

Scripture references the Father twelve times in the sixth chapter of Matthew. Let's look at a few of these as well as some other nearby references:

> Let your light shine before men in such a way that they may see your good works, and glorify your <u>Father</u> who is in heaven.
> Matthew 5:16

> 3 But when you give to the poor, do not let your left hand know what your right hand is doing, 4 so that your giving will be in secret; and your Father who sees what is done in secret will reward you.
> Matthew 6:3-4

²⁵ At that time Jesus said, "I praise You, Father, Lord of heaven and earth, that You have hidden these things from the wise and intelligent and have revealed them to infants. ²⁶ Yes, Father, for this way was well-pleasing in Your sight. ²⁷ All things have been handed over to Me by My Father; and no one knows the Son except the Father; nor does anyone know the Father except the Son, and anyone to whom the Son wills to reveal Him." Matthew 11:25-27

Matthew 11:25 is, in fact, one of the key themes of this book. God has hidden mysteries like this from the religious intellectuals of the day and given them to everyday people who simply seek Him diligently. Every time I teach this material, I am still blown away that God would reveal this to me. This verse also clearly shows that Jesus prays and talks to the Father.

Regarding order, we see Jesus and the Father in John 1:14 where the apostle says, "And the Word became flesh, and dwelt among us, and we saw His glory, glory as of the only begotten from the Father, full of grace and truth." This illustrates that Jesus received His glory from the Father, which means the Father is one hundred percent the source and origin of the salvation we enjoy in Christ. The Bible continually references the Father as the sender, the origin, and the giver.

It is worth noting that zero scriptural references define anyone beyond the Father. The Word of God says Jesus sits at the right hand of the Father, but to the left hand of the Father, the Word of God is silent. This states there is no one above Him. There is no one beyond Him. He is the source. There is nothing that does not find its source in the Father.

Snapshots of the Son

Now, let's look at scriptures validating the Son of God, Jesus Christ. There are hundreds of verses describing the Son as well. What we will look at here is merely a snapshot. When we examine the Matthew 3:16-17 passage, it is clear that the Father sends the Son to redeem His people:

> [16] After being baptized, Jesus came up immediately from the water; and behold, the heavens were opened, and he saw the Spirit of God descending as a dove and lighting on Him, [17] and behold, a voice out of the heavens said, "This is My beloved Son, in whom I am well-pleased."

The voice here is the Father speaking, and He's clearly talking about Jesus.

Contrast this with Matthew 4:3, which says, "And the tempter came and said to Him, 'If You are the Son of God, command that these stones become bread.'" Here, the devil is questioning the Sonship of Jesus, attempting to get our LORD to doubt who He is. We know the devil is a liar, but this is very interesting. In Matthew 4:3, we see the temptation of Christ, which took place just after His baptism. As Jesus came out of the water, the Father declared the Sonship of Christ. Shortly after that, much like with Eve in the Garden of Eden, the devil questions whether God's Word is true. Speaking to Jesus, satan doesn't say, "You are the Son of God." He says, "*If* You are the Son of God."

Now, look at the story of the demoniac, a man possessed by many demons. In Matthew 8:29, it says, "And they cried out, saying, 'What business do we have with each other, Son of God? Have You come here to torment us before the time?'" This was not your typical possession. Hundreds or maybe thousands of demons are declaring the Sonship of Christ here. They may not be as smart as the head devil, satan, but thousands of demons declaring the Sonship of Jesus is quite compelling. They were fully aware of His Sonship and operated in full and open rebellion to it.

In Matthew 4, satan is cunning in questioning the Sonship of God. In contrast, not long after in Matthew 8:29, there are perhaps thousands of demons declaring the Sonship of Jesus. Finally, in Matthew 12:8, Jesus declares *Himself* to be the LORD of the Sabbath. Calling Himself the LORD of the Sabbath is an entirely clear and deliberate claim to divinity. For most of His ministry on earth, Jesus consistently refers to Himself as the Son of Man. Here, however, He is laying a claim to His place as the second Person of the Trinity.

So we can see that demons professed Christ to be the Son of God, which fact Jesus also proclaimed to be true. What about His friends and those who knew Him best? Who did they say Jesus was? Look at Matthew 14:33: "And those who were in the boat worshiped Him, saying, 'You are certainly God's Son!'" His disciples, who spent so much time with Him, unquestionably got the message that Jesus is the Son of God. They believed it and declared it, and they would later end up dying for that belief.

Jesus once asked His disciples in Matthew 16:16 point-blank who they believed Him to be. In His typical boldness, Peter answered Him, "You are the Christ, the Son of the living God." Peter is just out with it; he has no filter. To

Peter's credit, Jesus affirms his declaration. Jesus did not directly say here that He is the Son of God, but He affirms the declaration of Peter, who called Him the Son of God. Peter effectively said (paraphrased), "You are the Christ. You are the Anointed One, the Son of the Living God."

Matthew goes on to tell us, "And Jesus said to him, 'Blessed are you, Simon Barjona, because flesh and blood did not reveal this to you, but My Father who is in heaven'" (Matthew 16:17). These are just a few of the hundreds of verses declaring the deity and Sonship of Jesus. There can be absolutely no mistake. The Father sent Jesus, His divine Son.

Snapshots of the Holy Spirit

Finally, let us look at a few scriptural snapshots that validate the powerful refreshment that is the Holy Spirit. Many verses describe the Holy Spirit as being sent by the Father through Jesus and describe Him being available to all after Pentecost (the arrival of the Holy Spirit in power). The Holy Spirit is the most mysterious member of the Trinity.

Romans 8:11 tells us that the same power that raised Jesus from the dead dwells inside the born-again believer in Jesus. That power in you is the Holy Spirit. Acts 1:8 says, "But you will receive power when the Holy Spirit has come upon you; and you shall be My witnesses both in Jerusalem, and in all Judea and Samaria, and even to the remotest part of the earth." The work of the Holy Spirit as a member of the Godhead is completely astounding. He moves into the spirit of man and binds us to God, guiding us, empowering us, and thereby transforming our former destiny into a heavenly destiny. When the veil of the temple was rent in two at the crucifixion of Christ, the Spirit of God checked out of the temple. On the day of Pentecost, the Spirit of God checked into the hearts of those who called on the name of Jesus for salvation.

We also see the Person of the Holy Spirit powerfully displayed through the doctrine of baptism. John the Baptist explained to his followers that he was only baptizing them with water. The baptism he provided was a baptism unto repentance. In Matthew 3:11, however, John speaks of a greater baptism to come: "As for me, I baptize you with water for repentance, but He who is coming after me is mightier than I, and I am not fit to remove His sandals; He will baptize you with the Holy Spirit and fire."

John's baptism was with water unto repentance, but Jesus baptizes with the Holy Spirit and the fire of God.

So John's baptism was with water unto repentance, but Jesus baptizes with the Holy Spirit and the fire of God. The Holy Spirit *indwells us with divine power* and the ability to literally walk as Jesus did and perform the works of Jesus and even beyond (John 14:12).

> [5] Jesus answered, "Truly, truly, I say to you, unless one is born of water and the Spirit he cannot enter into the kingdom of God. [6] That which is born of the flesh is flesh, and that which is born of the Spirit is spirit."
> John 3:5-6

John 14:26 says, "But the Helper, the Holy Spirit, whom the Father will send in My name, He will teach you all things, and bring to your remembrance all that I said to you." Do you see that? Jesus calls the Holy Spirit *the Helper*. The Helper, the Holy Spirit, whom—pay attention here—the Father sends through Jesus, will teach you all things and remind you of all the things Jesus said and taught. In John 15:26-27, Jesus comforts His disciples by saying:

> 26 When the Helper comes, whom I will send to you from the Father, *that is* the Spirit of truth who proceeds from the Father, He will testify about Me, 27 and you *will* testify also, because you have been with Me from the beginning.

The Holy Spirit is a gift from the Father, but God only made the Spirit available to everyone after the resurrection of Jesus. What about before the resurrection? The Word of God describes King Saul receiving the Spirit of God and then subsequently having it removed from him because of his disobedience. Likewise, King David receives the Spirit of God and then begs not to have the Holy Spirit removed from him when he sins with Bathsheba. Similarly, the Holy Spirit would move upon Samson (Judges 14:6 and 14:9). So the Holy Spirit has always been, but He has not always been available to all as He is to us today under a better covenant.

Acts 2:33 says, "Therefore having been exalted to the right hand of God, and having received from the Father the promise of the Holy Spirit, He has poured forth this which you both see and hear." At this point, Jesus is back in the throne room, and the Spirit of God has been sent to earth to live inside you. If you're born again, He's in you, and He's not going anywhere.

From the Big Picture to Snapshots

As we conclude this chapter, let's consider for a moment that when God chose to reveal His name to Moses in proto-Sinaitic pictographic Hebrew, 𐤉𐤄𐤅𐤄 He gave it in picture form. It is my belief that this was a picture of things that were *yet to happen.* We see symbolism and order of the picture distilled into the scriptural snapshots of the Father, the Son, and the Holy Spirit.

God uses a pattern of progressive revelation in the scriptures. The Father reveals all things according to His timeline as described by Jesus when He explains in detail what will come to pass in the last days (Matthew 24:36). No man knows when all the prophecies will be fulfilled, not even Jesus. Only the Father has the complete picture. The rest of us must look at the snapshots revealed in scripture to discover the majesty and wonder of the Three-In-One-God.

God uses a pattern of progressive revelation in the scriptures.

The backstory is now filled in. It is time to unveil the mystery and start unpacking the Tetragrammaton 𐤉𐤄𐤅𐤄, written as God gave it to Moses 3,500 years ago. There are four characters in the Tetragrammaton 𐤉𐤄𐤅𐤄. Three of them represent the elements of the Trinity as described in scripture: the Father, the Son, and the Holy Spirit. The fourth is the most surprising of all. Hidden in plain sight for centuries, we are now ready to reveal what has been lost. I must warn you that once you see this, you will never read scripture the same again.

The YOD
(Father)

As we learned in the previous chapter, the Trinity is comprised of the Father (*YOD*), the Son (*HEY*), and the Holy Spirit (*VAV*). We know the Father to be the first Person of the Trinity, and the *YOD* is the first character in the name of God 𐤉𐤅𐤄𐤉. In pictographic Hebrew (shortened version from now on), the symbol for *YOD* is a picture of an outstretched arm and a right hand 𐤉. If you've spent any time in church or reading the Bible, you've no doubt heard or read the phrase "the right hand of God" many times. Isn't it interesting that the right hand of God the Father is depicted in His name 𐤉𐤅𐤄𐤉? The pictographic representation of the Father's right hand is central to who He is, and truly, that is just scratching the surface. There is much more about the

YOD and how it represents the Father; I believe it will amaze you.

Let me begin by making a few statements, which we will confirm with scripture. First, in pictographic Hebrew, the *YOD* ⅃ character represents the concrete actions of giving, working, making, throwing, and casting. With the *YOD*'s pictorial representation being an outstretched arm ⅃, it represents the truth that God the Father is reaching out His right hand to work for the good of His people and to bless them. He never stops working, and He never ceases reaching out to you and me. Psalms 121:4 says, "Behold, He who keeps Israel will neither slumber nor sleep." He is always working for our good.

Moses Affirms the Imagery of God's Name

Deuteronomy 11:2 says, "Know this day that I *am* not *speaking* with your sons who have not known and who have not seen the discipline of the LORD your God—His greatness, His mighty hand and <u>His outstretched arm</u>." Bear in mind that we know the word "LORD" here is ⅃, so consider that Moses is literally the first person in the history of the world to see what the name of God ⅃ looks like when written down. Then Moses affirms in writing the concept of His mighty hand and outstretched arm on the written page. Doesn't the verse become far more awe-inspiring when we begin to understand the meaning behind the original pictographic Hebrew script?

God revealed His unspeakable name to Moses at a specific time and for a specific purpose, and Moses, according to the New Testament, had the skills and the training to "write these things down." Looking at the word pictures contained in the name of יהוה, Moses would begin to understand the fundamental implications of God's Holy name. As we've discussed, Hebrew was Moses' native language, so he would not have misunderstood the concrete imagery of the Father reaching down, creating, blessing, sustaining, working, and yes, sometimes even throwing. "As they fled from before Israel, *while* they were at the descent of Beth-horon, the LORD threw large stones from heaven on them as far as Azekah, and they died; *there were* more who died from the hailstones than those whom the sons of Israel killed with the sword" (Joshua 10:11).

Let's look at another depiction of יהוה in the Old Testament. Isaiah 28:2 describes the LORD יהוה as follows: "Behold, the Lord has a strong and mighty *agent*; as a storm of hail, a tempest of destruction, like a storm of mighty overflowing waters, He has cast *it* down to the earth with *His* hand." Do you see God reaching down, casting, throwing, and creating? These actions are part of who the Father is. He builds up the righteous and throws down the wicked. The right hand of God the Father is always working on behalf of those who love and honor Him, and He works to disrupt the plans of the wicked. Even in our sinful choices and actions, the Father is working all things together for our good.

The *YOD* in the New Testament

You may find it fascinating that God does not limit the imagery of the *YOD* to the Old Testament. In 1 Peter 5:6-7, Peter writes, "Therefore humble yourselves under the mighty hand of God, that He may exalt you at the proper time, casting all your anxiety on Him, because He cares for you." Since Peter writes of the "mighty hand of God," it is worth asking where he got such an idea. Well, Peter was a Jew, and Jews study the Torah, so he most likely got it from Moses. Peter was a disciple, or scholar—a *talmîḏ* in Hebrew—of *Jesus.* Contrary to the rough picture many paint of Peter, he was very devout. In fact, he would struggle with this strongly engrained religious mindset when he should have been entirely living under the new covenant of grace. The apostle Peter was a student of the Torah, and he knew his scriptures. So when Peter read the word LORD 𐤉𐤄𐤅𐤄, it is very possible he would still have had the generational, pictographic Hebrew concepts in his mind. I contend that since numerous scriptures illustrate the concept of the "mighty hand of God" being part of the very name of 𐤉𐤄𐤅𐤄, the pictorial representation was almost certainly handed down orally by the rabbis (teachers) of the Law. This means that speaking in these terms would have been second nature for a man (a *talmîḏ*) like Peter.

Now we know pictographic Hebrew is a script based on pictures, which are based on concrete ideas. These ideas are then inextricably woven into the scriptures. Later those pictures are translated into paleo-Hebrew, a phonic-based script (meaning letters represent sounds instead of representing ideas or things). From there, the ideas and concepts are translated yet again, this time into an Aramaic Hebrew script (also phonic in nature). We lose the pictographic script through all that translation, but the concepts are still there. The pictures are lost (until now), but the *meaning* remains.

Although it is possible that because the Hebrew language had transitioned from pictographic Hebrew to paleo-Hebrew to Aramaic script by the time Peter arrived on the scene, the concrete writing style of the pictographic Hebrew could have been lost on him. This seems unlikely, however, since he reiterates this same illustration of God's mighty hand. By Peter's time, the *meaning* of the right hand of God (the Father) was firmly established and taught.

The *YOD* is the Father

Over thousands of years, multiple authors reference God's (the Father's) right hand in many verses throughout scripture. How did so many people, at so many different times, remain consistent in their description of the Father? How did they receive inspiration regarding the right hand of God? Let's look at a few of these scriptures that show this consistency over so many hundreds of years:

> "Your right hand, O Lord, is majestic in power, Your right hand, O Lord, shatters the enemy" (Exodus 15:6).

> "You stretched out Your right hand, the earth swallowed them" (Exodus 15:12).

> "You have also given me the shield of Your salvation, and Your right hand upholds me; and Your gentleness makes me great" (Psalm 18:35).

> "Surely My hand founded the earth, and My right hand spread out the heavens; when I call to them, they stand together" (Isaiah 48:13).

> "Do not fear, for I am with you; do not anxiously look about you, for I am your God. I will strengthen you, surely I will help you, surely I will uphold you with My righteous right hand" (Isaiah 41:10).

> "The sound of joyful shouting and salvation is in the tents of the righteous; the <u>right hand</u> of the LORD does valiantly" (Psalm 118:15).

Are you seeing this? When the writers reference God (the Father), they prominently feature His right hand, yet the authors—Moses, David, and Isaiah—lived hundreds of years apart. Despite this, they all were keenly aware of the power and working of the right hand of God (the Father). By the way, the salvation of YHVH, which David writes about in the Psalm above, is Jesus. From Genesis to Malachi, the theme of the right hand and the outstretched arm applies to the Father. Through dozens of books, multiple authors, and hundreds of years, the theme does not change. There must be something to this. Only the inspiration of God could reveal this to the minds of men.

So we have learned that in pictographic Hebrew, the name of God 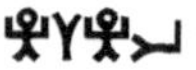 is literally a picture of the Trinity. We know God the Father is the first Person of the Trinity. We also know that the *YOD* is the first character of the name , therefore the *YOD* is a direct reference to God the Father. We see this concept originating in the earliest pages of scripture and carries on to the very last pages.

The YOD is a direct reference to God the Father.

As a quick side note, did you know there are no references to the left hand of God in scripture? So what or who is at the left hand of God? There is no authority or power to the left of the Father. In Jeremiah 10:6, the prophet declared, "There is none like You, O LORD."

The Father is the origin of all things. There is nothing to His left because all He has created flows out of His right hand.

How is it that the New Testament writers got so much inspiration related to the right hand of God, the Father, and never reference the left hand of God? I believe it is because time, matter, and even the universe itself begin with the Father. He is from everlasting to everlasting (Psalm 90:2), and His right hand is strong enough to hold all things together and work them out for the good of those who love Him. "And we know that God causes all things to work together for good to those who love God, to those who are called according to *His* purpose" (Romans 8:28).

> [18] I *pray that* the eyes of your heart may be enlightened, so that you will know what is the hope of His [the Father's] calling, what are the riches of the glory of His [the Father's] inheritance in the saints, [19] and what is the surpassing greatness of His [the Father's] power toward us who believe. *These are* in accordance with the working of the strength of His [the Father's] might [20] which He [the Father] brought about in Christ [the Son], when He [the Father] raised Him [the Son] from the dead and seated Him [the Son] at His [the Father's] <u>right hand</u> [*YOD*] in the heavenly *places*, [21] far above all rule and authority and power and dominion, and every name that is named, not only in this age but also in the one to come. Ephesians 1:18-21

We will look at Ephesians 1:20 more closely in the next few chapters, but for the moment, we will focus on the fact that the "He" in verse twenty is the Father. He—the Father—raised Him—Jesus—from the dead and seated Him—

Jesus—at His—the Father's—right hand. Are you seeing it? It's so simple and clear. *This* is the Tetragrammaton ✡Y✡⅃ in action.

In Matthew 6, Jesus' disciples ask Him to teach them to pray. It is a simple question displaying innocence and an eagerness to learn. Jesus must have been pleased with the question as He responded by providing explicit instructions on how to pray. His teaching applies not only to the original twelve disciples, but it is every bit as relevant to us today. You probably remember this teaching, but here is how Jesus taught them to pray in Matthew 6:9-13.

> [9] Pray, then, in this way: "Our Father who is in heaven, hallowed be Your name. [10] Your kingdom come. Your will be done, on earth as it is in heaven. [11] Give us this day our daily bread. [12] And forgive us our debts, as we also have forgiven our debtors. [13] And do not lead us into temptation, but deliver us from evil. [For Yours is the kingdom and the power and the glory forever. Amen.]"

Notice that Jesus begins His model prayer with "Our Father." This is profound! The Tetragrammaton, the unspeakable name of God ✡Y✡⅃, starts with the *YOD*. In the same way, our prayers must begin with *YOD*. He is our Father. He is first. He is the source. We will unveil this mystery bit by bit, but by the end of this book, you will see the power of the statement, "Our Father." We approach Him through the delegated authority of the name of Jesus, but we must begin by humbly addressing the Father (*YOD*).

Has anyone ever taught you to pray in this way? Do your prayers follow the model laid out by Jesus when He taught His disciples, as recorded in the above passage? All the teachings of Jesus are timeless, so how much more fundamental is His instruction on how we should pray? After all, if anyone knows how to speak to the Father, surely it is the only begotten Son of the Father? In Jesus, we can talk to the Father. As sons and daughters adopted into His family by the grace and blood of Jesus Christ, we can speak directly to *our* Father.

Only the Beginning

We have begun the process of closely analyzing the Tetragrammaton ✡Y✡⌐ and its component characters. I hope you are starting to feel the excitement of a long-held mystery. I promise you it only gets better. For now, let us review and meditate on the following realities:

- God's name is a name that both illustrates and describes the essence of The Godhead (Trinity). This name is ✡Y✡⌐.

- God first revealed this name to Moses. It contains four characters, and each of these four characters is profoundly powerful. Both God and Moses wrote the unspeakable name in a known script. Scripture and secular archaeology affirm that this script was likely pictographic Hebrew.

- The Tetragrammaton is a simple yet complete diagram of the Trinity and of Heaven's throne room. The Tetragrammaton is also a powerful evangelistic tool that reaches across cultural bounds and unlocks the gospel for people of every tribe, nation, and tongue. More about this later.

- The *YOD* is the first character in the unspeakable name of God. A simple picture of an outstretched arm and a right hand represent the *YOD*.

- The *YOD* represents the Father.

We've covered a lot of ground already, but as I keep promising, you haven't seen anything yet. As we step through the characters in the name of God, there are many more discoveries to make. God wrapped up an enormous amount of truth in each letter, so don't rush through these chapters. Instead, meditate on what you are reading. Savor the goodness of God as you begin to understand Him in new and beautiful ways. The *YOD* is the first character in the unspeakable name of God, and in so many ways, it is only the beginning.

Take a moment to pause and thank our Father (*YOD*) for His Word, open your favorite Bible app, and do a word search of the "right hand" of God.

The First HEY
(Jesus the Son)

I wonder what it felt like the first time Moses wrote down the name of God. Long before Moses ever wrote the name down, he had on two occasions seen the hand of God write ☥Y☥ᴗ. Have you ever wondered what the tablets of the Ten Commandments looked like? Often when you see the tablets represented in modern content, the words are either written in modern or paleo-Hebrew. These scripts were simply not used at the time of the Exodus.

In this chapter, we will look at the second character in the pictographic Hebrew name of God, which is the HEY. The most primitive form of the character is written in the image of a man with his arms outstretched ☥. The name of God occurs eight times in the Ten Commandments. When

Moses saw the hand of God draw the HEY, the man with outstretched arms, what was he thinking? He saw God write the first character as an outstretched right hand, and to this character's right is the image of a man with outstretched arms ⚲. What can this mean?

There are two things to consider as we meditate on this symbol. Since we read Hebrew from right to left, remember from the previous chapter that the *YOD* represents the Father. The second character, the *HEY*, therefore represents the Son, Jesus. As you know, there are two *HEY*s in ⚲Y⚲ꓶ, the unspeakable name of God. The *HEY* under discussion in this chapter is the *first HEY*.

To begin looking at the profound meaning of this character, the character HEY in pictographic Hebrew represents the concrete ideas of looking, beholding, or revealing. The first point to note is that when Jesus walked among us, He always revealed the Father to men. Look at the words of Jesus as recorded in John 14:9: "Jesus said to him, 'Have I been so long with you, and yet you have not come to know Me, Philip? He who has seen Me has seen the Father; how can you say, "Show us the Father"?"

We could say the *HEY* spent much of His ministry revealing the *YOD*.

Now consider that the Hebrew word for "behold" is *hinneh*[8], which appears 843 times in the Old Testament. This word often points to Jesus, and one example is the following: "Therefore the Lord Himself will give you a sign: Behold, a virgin will be with child and bear a son, and she will call His name Immanuel" (Isaiah 7:14).

In the New Testament, when John the Baptist saw Jesus approaching him at the Jordan River, he said much the same thing: "The next day he saw Jesus coming to him and said, 'Behold, the Lamb of God who takes away the sin of the world!'" (John 1:29). To me the symbolism of the second character in the name of God—a man with his arms stretched out ⵣ—is simple, concrete, and clear. Psalm 89:13 says, "You have a strong arm; Your hand is mighty, Your right hand is exalted." Likewise, as Mark 14:62 records it, "Jesus said, 'I am; and you shall see the Son of Man sitting at the right hand of power, and coming with the clouds of heaven.'" Who is the "Son of Man" other than Jesus Himself? Where is Jesus sitting? He is seated at the right hand of power. That right hand of power is none other than the Father ⵡ.

There are several other verses that display Jesus' divinity:

"<u>Behold</u>, the Lamb of God who takes away the sins of the world" (John 1:29).

"<u>Behold</u> the Lamb of God" (John 1:36).

"<u>Behold</u> the virgin shall be with child" (Matthew 1:23).

"<u>Behold</u>, your King is coming to you" (Matthew 21:5).

So let's review: God gave Himself a name, and we know His name has four characters—ⵣYⵣⵡ. These scriptures then imply that the mystery we are to behold, as declared by the prophets and Jesus, is that God is triune in the Old Testament and the New. When you begin to understand the pictographic Hebrew as a key to unlocking the Trinity, as you spend time with God in the scriptures, you will begin to see these images everywhere. Countless scriptures underscore the simple concrete positional statements of the pictographic Hebrew name of God.

Acts 2:33 states it crystal clear: "Therefore having been exalted to the right hand of God, and having received from the Father the promise of the Holy Spirit, He has poured forth this which you both see and hear." Note that, yet again, we see the entire Trinity in this single verse. Within these words, we see Jesus exalted to the right hand of the Father, and after receiving the Holy Spirit from the Father, Jesus pours out the Spirit on those who believe. Father, Son, and Holy Spirit are working together as one *to save, adopt, and empower us.* This is the name of God ﷲ in action.

The Cross in the Name of God ﷲ

When discussing the Trinity, there are two basic and obvious things we should remember. First, the second Person of the Trinity is God, who came to us as a man. The second obvious fact is that they stretched this man out on a Roman cross to pay the penalty of sin (which is death). Jesus submitted Himself to be crucified for the forgiveness of sins and the salvation of men. The second character in the pictographic Hebrew is the *HEY*—the image of a man with outstretched arms. This is an unmistakable representation of the Son, Jesus, who came to Earth as a man and was stretched out on a Roman cross as a sacrifice for our sins. We can say, therefore, that in the name of God, the first *HEY* literally defines Jesus as the salvation of ﷲ.

There are many Messianic prophecies that have been fulfilled through the ages, and the one Moses wrote in Exodus 6:3 reflects what we're discussing here. In the revelation of His name, ⸰⸰⸰⸰ God shows us that Jesus would come and sacrifice His life for ours.

The Only Begotten Son

As we know, Mary, Jesus' mother, became pregnant in a non-traditional way, without the help or intervention of any man. An angel of God told her exactly what to name the child, the same child she would later see stretched out on a cross. Is there a better or more precise picture of the person and work of Christ than a man with his arms stretched out ⸰⸰?

From what we can tell in scripture, Jesus grew up as a typical young Jewish man of His time. He did, of course, show a strong proclivity towards studying the Torah (Luke 2:49). There's no indication, however, that Jesus was overly rich or poor, and His life was much like that of every other child of His time. Jesus worked hard and lived in a simple community until He began His public ministry.

Suddenly, at the appointed moment, Jesus ascended from the waters of His baptism, and God the Father said, "This is My beloved Son, in whom I am well pleased" (Matthew 3:17). The Father calls Jesus, "My Son whom I love," and in doing so, the Father removes any doubt about the identity of Jesus. Jesus is God, just as He said He was, and there are mountains of verses in the Bible that prove this. Let's look at a few examples of scriptures that refer to the "Son of man" as "the Son of God":

For whoever is ashamed of Me and My words in this adulterous and sinful generation, the <u>Son of Man</u> will also be ashamed of him when He comes in the glory of His Father with the holy angels. Mark 8:38

"Which is easier, to say, 'Your sins have been forgiven you,' or to say, 'Get up and walk'? 'But, so that you may know that the <u>Son of Man</u> has authority on earth to forgive sins,'" He said to the paralytic, "'I say to you, get up, and pick up your stretcher and go home.'" Luke 5:23-24

Jesus heard that they had put him out, and finding him, He said, "Do you believe in the <u>Son of Man</u>?" He answered, "Who is He, Lord, that I may believe in Him?" Jesus said to him, "You have both seen Him, and He is the one who is talking with you." John 9:35-37

Therefore many other signs Jesus also performed in the presence of the disciples, which are not written in this book; but these have been written so that you may believe that Jesus is the Christ, the <u>Son of God</u>; and that believing you may have life in His name. John 20:30-31

And we know that the <u>Son of God</u> has come, and has given us understanding so that we may know Him who is true; and we are in Him who is true, in <u>His Son</u> Jesus Christ. This is the true God and eternal life. 1 John 5:20).

The angel answered and said to her, "The Holy Spirit will come upon you, and the power of the Most High will overshadow you; and for that reason the holy Child shall be called the <u>Son of God</u>." Luke 1:35

The Word of God makes no effort to hide the fact Jesus is indeed the Son of God. He is unmistakably the second Person of the Trinity. I believe He is depicted as the second figure in the name of God, 𐤅𐤉𐤄𐤄. God became one of us to save and adopt us, just as His name declares.

Hopefully, you see now that Jesus, the second Person of the Trinity, is clearly depicted in the second character of God's unspeakable name, 𐤅𐤉𐤄𐤄. Stick with me, and we'll see so much more. The name of God 𐤅𐤉𐤄𐤄 is not only the key to understanding the Trinity but even contains the gospel in only four short characters. To discover how, you'll need to keep reading. First, though, we must see if the Holy Spirit, the third Person of the Trinity, is also hidden within the unspeakable name of God. That's where we are going next.

The Word of God makes no effort to hide the fact Jesus is indeed the Son of God.

The VAV
(Holy Spirit)

7.

So far, we've found both the Father and the Son within the characters of God's unspeakable name, 𐤉𐤄𐤅𐤄. In scripture, the Holy Spirit follows Jesus in God's redemptive story of humanity. Can we find this truth within the name of God as well?

The third character in the pictographic Hebrew name of God is the *VAV* **Y**. So in the first three characters of 𐤉𐤄𐤅𐤄, we find the *YOD*, the *HEY*, and the *VAV*. The pictographic Hebrew character for the *VAV* is that of a *tent stake* **Y**. In Hebrew, the *VAV* represents the concrete ideas of adding, binding, and sealing. One thing to bear in mind is that tent stakes are driven downward into the ground with power and purpose, with the function of securing a tent. If you've ever driven a stake into the ground to secure a tent, you know it provides a sturdy defense against powerful winds. The tent is secure and is able to withstand the winds when they come.

Since Hebrew is read from right to left, the *VAV* is to the right of the *HEY*. I present a case that the *VAV* character **Y** represents the Holy Spirit. I will admit the tent peg imagery was a bit mysterious at first. In fact, it took significant time in prayer and meditation to unveil this part of the mystery. Nevertheless, I am subsequently convinced the tent peg is a uniquely practical and thoroughly concrete representation of the Holy Spirit.

The Pictographic Hebrew character for the VAV is that of a tent stake, and it represents the Holy Spirit.

The Strength of the Tent Peg

At first, one could ask, "Why on Earth would God represent His Spirit as a tent peg? **Y**" On the surface, it seems like a good question. To connect the symbol of a tent peg to the Holy Spirit may appear a little far-fetched but recall the basic purpose of a tent peg we addressed above. Then ask yourself why a tent needs pegs at all. The answer, of course, is *wind!* In the Old Testament, the word for Holy Spirit is *ruah*[9]. It is a feminine noun that means wind, breath, exhalation, and blast. In the New Testament, the word for the Holy Spirit is *pneuma*[10]. It is a neuter noun and means breath, blast, breeze, or Spirit. There is no direct character for the idea of "Spirit" or "Powerful Wind" in pictographic

Hebrew, so to use the tent peg to represent binding and powerful wind makes sense.

The Wind of God

The Book of Acts 2:2 describes the coming of the Holy Spirit in this way: "And suddenly there came from heaven a noise like a violent rushing wind, and it filled the whole house where they were sitting." Although that scripture was likely written in Greek, I'll show you that the concept is present in the Old Testament too. How, then, would an ancient Hebrew writer represent a violent, rushing wind? Since wind is invisible, it makes sense that a tent stake—the *VAV*—would be a good way to suggest the concrete idea of a strong, violent wind. Ask anyone who has ever put up a tent when a strong wind kicks up; your first thought will be about the tent pegs.

As mentioned earlier, in the Old Testament, the Hebrew word for the Spirit of God (the Holy Spirit) is *ruah and* is defined as "breath, wind, spirit." The passage of Genesis 1:2 states, "The earth was formless and void, and darkness was over the surface of the deep, and the Spirit of God was moving over the surface of the waters." The Spirit of God, or *Ruah*, moved over the surface of the waters. "Then the Lord God formed man of dust from the ground, and breathed into his nostrils the breath of life; and man became a living being" (Genesis 2:7). Can you see it? From these passages, we can conclude that it is the breath of God, the *Ruah*—the Holy Spirit of God—that brings man to life both physically and spiritually.

Therefore, I present the truth that the *Ruah*, the Spirit of God, the third Person of the Trinity, is the *VAV*—

represented as a tent peg **Y** in the unspeakable name of God. In Christ, it is He Who indwells us, gives us new life, and connects us to the power of God.

The *Ruah* and *Pneuma*

Much like *ruah,* the basic meaning of *pneuma,* the Greek word for the Holy Spirit in the New Testament, is wind or a blast of air. Both words contain a secondary meaning— the breath of life. If you've ever worked in a garage, you've probably used *pneumatic* tools. In factories, they use *pneumatic* cylinders. This is the idea behind the word. *Pneuma* is the Greek word for powerful air. We're not talking about a gentle breeze; think of compressed, concentrated, forceful air.

"Now the birth of Jesus Christ was as follows: when His mother Mary had been betrothed to Joseph, before they came together she was found to be with child by the Holy Spirit" (Matthew 1:18). Here in the historical story, we find Mary to be with child by the Holy Spirit, the Holy *Pneuma.* Mary was pregnant by the concentrated focus of the Holy Spirit of God, who breathed the second Person of the Trinity into a virgin's womb.

The Tent Peg

Getting back to the concrete idea of the tent peg, let us look at a few scriptural examples of the tent peg to see if it has any potential connection to the Person of the Holy Spirit. The tent peg shows up in the Old Testament, in a passage about the tribe of Judah, in Zechariah 10:4: "From them will come the cornerstone, from them the tent peg, from them the bow of battle, from them every ruler, *all* of them together." Scripture is clear that Jesus is the cornerstone, and He even refers to Himself as the cornerstone, but how about the tent peg? Who is this tent peg, and where did Zechariah get this idea? Is it possible it was from the apparent message contained within the name of ✡Y✡ᴚ? Also, notice the logical progression Zechariah leads us through, from the cornerstone on to the tent peg. Jesus came first: His incarnation, life, death, and resurrection. Then, the Holy Spirit is sent once Jesus completes His mission on Earth.

The *VAV* follows the *HEY*.

Jesus refers to Himself as the cornerstone in Matthew 21:42:

> Jesus said to them, "Did you never read in the Scriptures, 'THE STONE WHICH THE BUILDERS REJECTED, THIS BECAME THE CHIEF CORNER *stone*; THIS CAME ABOUT FROM THE LORD, AND IT IS MARVELOUS IN OUR EYES'?"

Here, Jesus is quoting Psalm 118:22-23. Notices He refers to Himself as the cornerstone, not the tent peg. By this, we know the tent peg Zechariah speaks of is not Jesus. The tent peg comes after Jesus, just as it appears ✡Y✡ᴚ. Again, the progression flows from the cornerstone to the tent peg. It flows from the *YOD* to the *HEY* to the *VAV*. The progression is from the Father to Jesus to the Holy Spirit.

Do you remember the story of Deborah in Judges 4? Deborah is the judge of all of Israel. During her tenure, Sisera, the commander of the Canaanite armies, attacks Israel. Despite being severely outnumbered and out-armed, the LORD helps Israel rout their enemy. As Israel is destroying the Canaanite army in battle, Sisera runs for his life and hides in the tent of Jael. Now Jael was the wife of Heber the Kenite, and Heber had a treaty with Sisera, so the Canaanite King assumed he would be safe there.

Jael subsequently gave the exhausted Sisera some milk, and after drinking it, he fell into a deep sleep. While Sisera slept, Jael took a tent peg and drove it straight through his head and into the ground. Now with this story in mind, let's fast forward about a thousand years to when Paul penned his letter to the church in Rome. He wrote, "For if you are living according to the flesh, you must die; but if by the Spirit [the *Pneuma*] you are putting to death the deeds of the body, you will live" (Romans 8:13). God's Holy Spirit, the *VAV* or the tent peg, drives power down from Heaven and puts our enemy, which is sin, to death in the believer's body made from earth. Your will plus God's Holy Spirit is a deadly combination for killing sin in the life of the born-again believer.

Your will plus God's Holy Spirit is a deadly combination for killing sin.

The Holy Spirit Follows Jesus

The post-resurrection ministry of Jesus ends with the firm command to stay in Jerusalem. Earlier, Christ had told His disciples, "But the Helper, the Holy Spirit, whom the Father will send in My name, He will teach you all things, and bring to your remembrance all that I have said to you" (John 14:26). Then, after His resurrection, Jesus gathered the disciples together and commanded them, "not to leave Jerusalem, but to wait for what the Father had promised, 'Which,' *He said*, 'you heard from Me'" (Acts 1:4). A little later, Jesus said to them, "But you will receive power when the Holy Spirit has come upon you; and you shall be My witnesses both in Jerusalem, and in all Judea and Samaria, and even to the remotest part of the earth" (Acts 1:8). What is the implication of this? Jesus was leaving His earthly ministry but was about to send the Holy Spirit to take His place. The Holy Spirit, the *VAV*, followed the Son, the *HEY*. This is precisely the message we find in the unspeakable name of God, 𐤉𐤄𐤅𐤄. Romans 8:11 says, "But if the Spirit of Him who raised Jesus from the dead dwells in you, He who raised Christ Jesus from the dead will also give life to your mortal bodies through His Spirit who dwells in you."

In plain English, the implications are immense. The Holy Spirit, the tent peg, comes in power and binds the born-again believer to Jesus Christ. God's Spirit came from Heaven, powerfully rushing to Earth in Acts 2, breathing new life into our spirits, and securing (sealing) us to our LORD and Savior, Jesus. Ephesians 1:13 tells us, "In Him, you also, after listening to the message of truth, the gospel of your salvation having also believed, you were sealed in Him with the Holy Spirit of promise." The Holy Spirit is as gentle and comforting as a cooing dove, but don't be mistaken even for a second. As I mentioned earlier in this chapter, all that surrounds the powerful Spirit of God is highly mysterious. Take a slow walk through 1 Corinthians 14 and Romans 8, and you will see that there is immense power available to those who are "in Christ."

The Holy Spirit is the sealing force between the glorified Christ and His people, the Church.

As a quick review, remember what we have now uncovered in the unspeakable name of God, יהוה. The tent peg Y is the pictographic Hebrew character for the *VAV*. As the *VAV* is in the third position of the pictographic Hebrew יהוה, it references the third Person of the Trinity, the Holy Spirit. Hidden in that wonderful name יהוה, we have found the Father (*YOD*), Son (*HEY*), and Holy Spirit (*VAV*). Are you seeing this? We find the whole of the Trinity and the gospel of God's redemption of humanity in the pictographic Hebrew name of God יהוה! Can it get any better than this? It can, it does, and it will blow your mind!

The Second
Hey

8.

In any nation on Earth, if you are caught breaking the law and a police officer points a gun at you, you put your hands up, regardless of nationality, culture, background, or language. People understand that putting your hands up is a universal symbol of surrender. In the western movies I enjoyed as a boy, the guy with the white hat would point his gun at the guy with the black hat and say something like, "Reach for the stars," or "Stick 'em up!" declaring the bad guy was out of options and had to raise his hands in surrender. Raised hands are a universal posture of surrender.

A second and no less pertinent interpretation of raised hands is that of praise and celebration. Think of the reaction at any sporting event when a team scores. As the ball enters the goalmouth, half the stadium automatically jumps to their feet with their hands in the air. The same thing occurs as a quarterback completes the game-winning touchdown. Likewise, as a ball flies through the hoop and the buzzer sounds, people jump up and raise their hands.

Some of you may know the feeling when the Holy Spirit begins to rise inside of you while experiencing moving worship music; your hands automatically go up because the natural posture of worship is to raise your hands. I remember how odd it seemed to me the first time I ever saw a man in the congregation worship God organically like this. As he stood with both hands raised to Heaven, in blissful abandon, I remember thinking, "Boy, that's strange." It was unsettling but powerful for a guy from a fundamentalist culture. In our little country church, this just was not done. This man had his hands raised in both surrender *and* praise; it moved me. Little did I know at that time that it was a beautiful representation of the second *Hey*.

Having walked through the first three characters in the pictographic Hebrew name of God, we have seen that the *Yod* ⤙ is a representation of the Father, the *Hey* 𐤄—a man with his arms outstretched—represents the Son, and the *Vav* Y—the tent peg driven in power—represents the Holy Spirit. Now we come to the fourth character in the unspeakable name of God, which happens to be another *Hey* 𐤄, also represented in the pictographic Hebrew as a man with his arms stretched out. What could it mean?

The Mystery of the Second Hey

For me, two critical questions emerge from this fourth character—the second *Hey*. The first question is this,

"Why would a triune God represent Himself with a four-character name ?"

The second question is, "Why is the *Hey* character , the character representing the Son, repeated?"

You may remember that the character *Hey* translates as "to look, behold, or reveal." Now recall John the Baptist saying, "Behold, the Lamb of God who takes away the sin of the world!" (John 1:29). When Jesus approached him, John said (paraphrased), "<u>Look</u>, behold, <u>the Lamb of God</u>!" As we discussed in Chapter 6, in the *Hey* representing Jesus, this "look" or "behold" is very logical. The outstretched arms being a picture of the cross, the position with reference to the Father, this all makes sense. This second *Hey*, however, is more complex, being almost as mysterious as the *Vav*. While understanding how the picture of a tent peg represents the Holy Spirit makes sense in hindsight, it was, at first, a mystery needing to be uncovered. Likewise, with the second *Hey*, we have another mystery requiring investigation.

Victory in Surrender

To examine the second *Hey*, I will take a different approach. I will provide the conclusion first, then give you a moment to let it sink in. The conclusion is this: when God disclosed His name to Moses in the fourteenth century BC in pictographic Hebrew, He was revealing a picture of the adoption of the born-again believer. This means that the second *Hey* in the pictographic Hebrew name of YHVH *is you!* To put it another way, all born-again believers are portrayed within the name of God. Our place of adoption by the Trinity was declared 3,500 years ago.

To begin, I want to take you back to the Exodus from Egypt and the story of Moses at Rephidim. The Lord told Moses that Pharaoh would let the Israelites go under compulsion: "Then the LORD said to Moses, 'Now you shall see what I will do to Pharaoh; for under <u>compulsion</u> he will let them go, and under <u>compulsion</u> he will drive them out of his land'" (Exodus 6:1). The Hebrew words for "under compulsion" reference the strong right hand of God (*yā<u>d</u>*[11] *ḥāzāq*[12]). Considering this, we see God was telling Moses that Pharaoh would let the people go because the right hand of God would compel him to do so.

The second Hey in the Pictographic Hebrew name of YHVH is you!

As you might imagine, the period between the Exodus and the time the Israelites came into the Promised Land was full of drama. Early in this drama, we find the record of the Amalekites coming out to battle the Israelites at Rephidim:

> [11] So it came about when Moses held his hand up, that Israel prevailed, and when he let his hand down, Amalek prevailed. [12] But Moses' hands were heavy. Then they took a stone and put it under him, and he sat on it; and Aaron and Hur supported his hands, one on one side and one on the other. Thus his hands were steady until

the sun set. ¹³ So Joshua overwhelmed Amalek and his people with the edge of the sword. Exodus 17:11-13

Moses overwatched this very first battle the children of Israel had to fight. The great rabbinical irony here is that as long as Moses' hands were up, *surrendering to* and *worshipping* God 𐤉𐤄𐤅𐤄, the people of God were victorious over their enemy. When Moses lowered his hands, the enemy began gaining ground. The picture God gives us in Exodus 17 is that when we surrender to and worship Him, we remain victorious.

At this point, I want to talk about our path to adoption into the family of God. Note that it is always a moment of surrender that marks our adoption. There is a moment in the born-again believer's life when we must put our hands up and surrender to Christ. The prophet Joel says it this way:

> ³² And it will come about that whoever calls on the name of the LORD will be delivered; for on Mount Zion and in Jerusalem there will be those who escape, as the LORD has said, even among the survivors whom the LORD calls.
> Joel 2:32

It is worth noting that Joel speaks the name of God 𐤉𐤄𐤅𐤄. Quoting the prophet Joel, Paul repeats this idea, "For 'WHOEVER WILL CALL ON THE NAME OF THE LORD WILL BE SAVED'" (Romans 10:13). What we see here is the moment of surrender, the moment in the life of the born-again believer where their hands go up in surrender, and they begin to worship.

Jesus, the source of our salvation, urged the crowds to find rest in Him:

²⁸ Come to Me, all who are weary and heavy-laden, and I will give you rest. ²⁹ Take My yoke upon you and learn from Me, for I am gentle and humble in heart, and YOU WILL FIND REST FOR YOUR SOULS. ³⁰ For My yoke is easy and My burden is light.
Matthew 11:28-30

I want to zero in on the part of this passage where Jesus says, "Come to Me, all who are weary and heavy-laden." It is in this surrender that we come to Christ, find salvation, and therefore rest. Remember, the Prodigal Son tried to do everything to please his fleshly desires, and when everything he thought mattered crashed down around him, he returned to his father and found love. This is the story of the believer. This is the story of the second *Hey*. It is the affirmation of our adoption.

The story of the second Hey is the affirmation of our adoption.

This adoption begins with our surrender, and our worship and praise flow out of our adoption. As the apostle Paul puts it, "The secrets of his heart are disclosed; and so he will fall on his face and worship God, declaring that God is certainly among you" (1 Corinthians 14:25). After this moment of surrender comes a moment of worship.

Do you remember when you were first born again, that first-love feeling, that moment of surrender immediately followed by praise as the heavy burden of sin was removed? You found rest after your surrender, and you couldn't have loved and worshiped God more in that moment. Philippians 3:3 says, "For we are the <u>true</u>

circumcision, who worship in the Spirit of God and glory in Christ Jesus and put no confidence in the flesh." The pictorial representation of the *Hey* beautifully depicts the experience of the born-again adopted believer. It is the picture of surrender and worship.

I, therefore, contend that when you examine the picture of the Tetragrammaton 𐤄𐤅𐤄𐤉 in pictographic Hebrew, you're looking at a picture of the throne room of Heaven. You're seeing God the Father on His throne. To His right is Jesus, the Messiah, born as a man, surrendering to His Father in death and worship. To Christ's right is the Holy Spirit, come to bring the power of 𐤄𐤅𐤄𐤉 to earth for mankind, and to the right of the Holy Spirit is the Bride of Christ—the second *Hey*—the born-again adopted believer. The location of the second *Hey* in the name of God depicts the binding (sealing) of the believer to the Father through the blood of Jesus and the power of the Holy Spirit.

The Holy Spirit you received, flowing from the Godhead, seals your adoption into the family of God, anchoring you firmly to resist any storm this world can present. Paul explains this in Romans 8:15: "For you have not received a spirit of slavery leading to fear again, but you have received a spirit of adoption as sons by which we cry out, 'Abba! Father!'" The Spirit you receive does not enslave you to live in fear; instead, He brings about your adoption into sonship. By Him, like Jesus, we cry, "Abba! Father!" When we surrender to God, we become His adopted children; indeed, even joint heirs with Christ, and *nothing* can ever take away our position:

³⁸ For I am convinced that neither death, nor life, nor angels, nor principalities, nor things present, nor things to come, nor powers, ³⁹ nor height, nor depth, nor any other created thing, will be able to separate us from the love of God, which is in Christ Jesus our Lord. Romans 8:38-39

The *Vav*, this powerful tent peg driven from Heaven into the spirits of men, binds and holds us to God, affirming our position as sons of God. From this perspective, 𐤅𐤄𐤅𐤉 is nothing less than a picture of the gospel: a picture of the second *Hey* worshiping—surrendering to the Godhead—bound to the Trinity through the Holy Spirit.

Romans 8:11 tells us, "But if the Spirit of Him who raised Jesus from the dead dwells in you, He who raised Christ Jesus from the dead will also give life to your mortal bodies through His Spirit who dwells in you." We are the adopted children of God *because* the Spirit of God 𐤅𐤄𐤅𐤉 lives within us. The Spirit of God lives inside us the same way God 𐤅𐤄𐤅𐤉 added humanity to the Trinity through Jesus. This wondrous work is nothing less than 𐤅𐤄𐤅𐤉 filling humanity with His deity through the indwelling of His Holy Spirit. As 2 Corinthians 4:7 states, "But we have this treasure in earthen vessels, so that the surpassing greatness of the power will be of God and not from ourselves."

We are the adopted children of God because the Spirit of God lives within us.

Destined for Sonship

As I'm sure you'll now agree, the name of God has many facets. Just as 𐤅𐤄𐤅𐤉 serves as a picture of the gospel, the pictographic name of God displays the original condition of man. Before the Fall, Adam was welcome in the presence of the LORD. This picture of the second *Hey* included in the name of God 𐤉𐤄𐤅𐤄 is a picture of *shalom*[13] (peace) restored. Before the stain of sin began to set on His beautiful creation, God 𐤉𐤄𐤅𐤄 declared His intention to redeem men and return them to the state of "GOD WITH US" (Matthew 1:23). The same *shalom*—the same completeness, soundness, welfare, and peace Adam experienced with God before sin—returns to the born-again believer through Christ's surrender in crucifixion and the subsequent power of the Holy Spirit as He was sent to earth.

When God revealed His name to Moses, He gave Moses a powerful prophecy of redemption. We were always destined to return to *shalom* (peace) with God 𐤉𐤄𐤅𐤄. As Ephesians 1:5 says, "He predestined us to adoption as sons through Jesus Christ to Himself, according to the kind intention of His will." If that still doesn't convince you, consider Romans 8:29: "For those whom He foreknew, He also predestined <u>to become</u> conformed to the image of His Son, so that He would be the firstborn among many brethren." The essence of these verses in Ephesians and Romans is hotly debated by mainstream denominations. What if these verses—verses that fueled the Calvinism versus Arminianism debate and caused many arguments over the centuries—are not what we thought them to be? To put it plainly, the second *Hey* in the name of God is a picture of the reality that everyone is predestined for adoption. The Apostle Paul clarifies this for us in Galatians 3:26-28:

²⁶ For you are all sons of God through faith in Christ Jesus. ²⁷ For all of you who were baptized into Christ have clothed yourselves with Christ. ²⁸ There is neither Jew nor Greek, there is neither slave nor free man, there is neither male nor female; for you are all one in Christ Jesus.

This scripture is also crystal clear that everyone is born with a free will. Like much rabbinical teaching, it allows for both things to be true. Yes, God is sovereign, and yes, I have the free will to make my own choices. Both things are true.

Putting It All together

Now we see the second *Hey* is a picture of us—you and me and all born-again believers—resting at the right hand of Jesus, filled with His Holy Spirit, adopted by the Father, and living in peace with the Trinity. This *is the gospel.* Jesus, represented in the first *Hey* of God's name, tells us in Luke 10:22, "All things have been handed over to Me by My Father, and no one knows who the Son is except the Father, and who the Father is except the Son, and anyone to whom the Son wills to reveal <u>Him</u>." Remember again that the *Hey* means to *behold* or *reveal.* Through the blood of Jesus and the power of the Holy Spirit, the glory of the Trinity is revealed to us, and we are revealed to the Trinity. In this, we see that one of the Son's functions is to reveal us to the Father.

We have also been through the historical progression of the Hebrew language and understand that God has a real, proper noun name. I have carefully unpacked each character in the name of God 𐤉𐤄𐤅𐤄 and provided scripture references supporting my conclusions. As we arrived at the fourth character, we discovered that God predestined us for adoption; God's plan has always been to love us, adopt us, and return us to peace with the Trinity.

Now we will move into the application of all we've learned and process how to deal with this information. First, we will consider how for 2,000 years, we as the Church have missed the fundamental truth that the name of God is the gospel. Next, we will consider the practical application of how the name of God is the picture of the Trinity and a picture of the adoption of humanity by the Godhead. Finally, we will consider how we have overlooked the name of God as a diagram of prayer and the key to unlocking the Kingdom of Heaven. As we move into the application of this knowledge, allow me to pose one more question worth pondering.

Just How Adopted Are You?

Once, after sharing this information in a presentation, I asked a prominent theologian a simple question: "Just how adopted are you?" Pointing at the fourth person, the fourth character, the second *Hey,* I asked,

"Are you this adopted?"

"Yes, I am," he replied.

What does this mean? If you are still unsure of how adopted you are, consider this scripture carefully:

> [4] But God, being rich in mercy, because of His great love with which He loved us, [5] even when we were dead in our transgressions, made us alive together with Christ (by grace you have been saved), [6] and raised us up with Him, and seated us with Him in the heavenly places in Christ

Jesus, [7] so that in the ages to come He might show the surpassing riches of His grace in kindness toward us in Christ Jesus.
Ephesians 2: 4-7

Imagine God comes to earth and dies for you so His Spirit can inhabit you, then imagine the blood of Christ places God's Spirit inside you. Finally, imagine the Almighty God predestined a seat of authority for you in the very throne room of Heaven. Now realize all these things are true and revealed in the name of God 𐤉𐤄𐤅𐤄. Through His Holy Spirit, by the blood of Jesus freely given for us, we are the adopted sons and daughters of God 𐤉𐤄𐤅𐤄—*joint heirs with Jesus Christ.*

In the following chapters, I will discuss the application of this reality, how it can play out in your life and ministry, the role it can play in evangelism, and how it can become a God-ordained, God-revealed systematic theology for you to gain deeper insight into the scriptures. I hope to give you a place to put your feet; a systematic theology so simple, so basic, almost child-like. I hope this reality can help you understand your value to the Father, your place in the Kingdom of Heaven, and the peace of being adopted, raised up, and seated with Him in heavenly places in Christ Jesus.

The Gospel within
God's Name

The word *gospel* gets flung around Christian circles quite a bit these days. It is a label that is slapped on everything from teaching to mission to general ministry, yet when I ask a thirty-year veteran of the Christian faith to describe the gospel, I often get a blank stare. Very few people really know its meaning. It is one of those words that gets used a lot yet is rarely understood. So I ask you now . . . *what is the gospel?*

The Greek word for gospel is *euangelion*[14] and it literally means "good news" or "good message." One of my mentors, Kenny, describes the gospel as "Jesus dead, buried and raised." Another of my favorite Bible teachers describes the gospel as "The almost-too-good-to-be-true news." If I stopped you on the street and asked you to define what the gospel is, what would you say? If you stopped me on the street and asked me the same question, I would draw you a picture. This picture 𐤉𐤅𐤄𐤉 would be the same picture God drew for Moses 3,500 years ago. This picture contains the entirety of the gospel in four characters. The name of God is a diagram of the gospel: a schematic of God's love, God's will, God's salvation, God's power, and, oh yes, your adoption. Stick with me for the rest of this chapter and I will show you in detail how to digest this for yourself and then share it with others.

Yod

Let's start with the Father depicted by the *Yod* ⏌ character. All the way to the far right of God's name, 𐤉𐤅𐤄𐤉, is one of

Because of the Father's unfathomable lovingkindness, He has always planned to adopt you.

an outstretched arm and a right hand. If you wish to share the gospel with anyone, this character is easy to draw and illustrates the Father is a *giver*. The Father is also a sender, a creator, and a caster. In the full biblical context, the Father is the origin of *chesed*[15], meaning "goodness, kindness, faithfulness." *Chesed* is the word used most often in the Old Testament to describe the lovingkindness of the Father.

Because of the Father's unfathomable lovingkindness, He has always planned to adopt you. Saying He loves you doesn't quite capture His heart for you. Saying He adores you doesn't even do His love justice. The Father is the origin of love, He is love. Love, the very foundation of the gospel message—the almost-too-good-to-be-true news—is found in John 3:16-17. The guy who made dirt and lit the sun on fire loves you!

> [16] For God so loved the world, that He gave His only begotten Son, that whoever believes in Him shall not perish, but have eternal life. [17] For God did not send the Son into the world to judge the world, but that the world might be saved through Him.

Do you see the right hand of the Father in these verses? He gave, He sent, and most of all, He *loved*. Whether you are a believer or not, be entirely assured that the Father loves you. This is further shown by asking whose idea it was to send the Son. These verses answer that question: it was the Father. The Son was sent in His Father's perfect will. God has loved you from before you were even conceived in this natural world, and He devised a plan to connect you to Himself for eternity through adoption.

We find evidence for this truth in Ephesians 1:5, which says, "He predestined us to <u>adoption</u> as sons through Jesus Christ to Himself, according to the <u>kind intention</u> of His will." The "He" here is the Father. God always intended to adopt you as His child, and He sent His only begotten Son, Jesus, because He loves you and wants to adopt you as His child.

Hey

Now let's look at the second character, the *Hey* 𐤄. Again, notice the flow of the pictographic gospel is from right to left. The *Hey* is the second character of 𐤄𐤅𐤄𐤉. In eternity past, the Son was, in the present, He *is*. He was and is in perfect harmony with the Father. John 1:14 says, "And the Word became flesh, and dwelt among us, and we saw His glory, glory as of the only begotten from the Father, full of grace and truth." The Word of God is very clear that Jesus is greatly loved by His Father. Matthew 3:17 tells us, "And behold, a voice out of the heavens said, 'This is <u>My beloved Son</u>, in whom I am well-pleased.'"

I find a no more straightforward way to share the gospel. If you can make a simple drawing of the *Hey* 𐤄—a man with his arms outstretched, you can share with your loved one that Jesus, the salvation of 𐤄𐤅𐤄𐤉, was sent by the Father, became a man, put on a *meat suit (humanity and flesh)*—and came down here to live and suffer with us to provide the perfect sacrifice. By this, the salvation of God came through a blood sacrifice. "And according to the Law, *one may* almost *say*, all things are cleansed with blood, and without shedding of blood there is no forgiveness" (Hebrews 9:22).

Similarly, Acts 4:10-12 says:

[10] Let it be known to all of you and to all the people of Israel, that by the name of Jesus Christ the Nazarene, whom you crucified, whom God raised from the dead— by this name this man stands here before you in good health. [11] He is the STONE WHICH WAS REJECTED by you, THE BUILDERS, but WHICH BECAME THE CHIEF CORNER stone. [12] And there is salvation in no one else; for there is no other name under heaven that has been given among men by which we must be saved.

This scripture proves that your salvation comes from the Father through Jesus alone. There is no other way, no other faith system. All roads do not lead to divine adoption. Jesus alone does.

While the Father sent Jesus, He came to die willingly because He, too, loves us. Jesus, as the writer of Hebrews explains, was very much human: "For we do not have a high priest who cannot sympathize with our weaknesses, but <u>One who has been tempted in all things as *we are, yet* without sin</u>" (Hebrews 4:15). Jesus felt the sting of human suffering and the sheer agony of the cross in an all too real way. Make this point when you draw the man with His arms stretched out. God chose to suffer for you so you could be adopted.

Jesus was immensely distressed as He faced the purchase price of our salvation. Matthew 26:39 tells us, "And He went a little beyond *them*, and fell on His face and prayed, saying, 'My Father, if it is possible, let this cup pass from Me; yet not as I will, but as You will.'" This scripture shows Jesus is fully God and was fully man, yet Hebrews 12:2 tells us that Jesus is "the author and perfecter of faith, who for the joy set before Him <u>endured the cross, despising the shame</u>, and has sat down at the <u>right hand</u> of the throne of God."

Look at everything encapsulated in that verse: Jesus endured the cross with His arms outstretched ✸, and He sat down at the right hand of the Father ✶. That is precisely where the pictographic name of God shows Him ✸Y✸✶. Death died that day, not Jesus! Shame, guilt, condemnation, and the power of hell died that day. Not Jesus! "<u>He is not here, for He has risen</u>, just as He said. Come, see the place where He was lying" (Matthew 28:6). The picture of Jesus being the *Hey* in God's name is not a stretch at all. It is everywhere in the New

Testament. The name of God, 𐤉𐤄𐤅𐤄 , is a clear picture of the gospel, and the first *Hey* in this name represents Jesus, a man with his arms outstretched, sent by the Father. Even His name *Yeshua* means the literal salvation of God 𐤉𐤄𐤅𐤄.

Vav

Lastly, note that as we teach the gospel from the 𐤉𐤄𐤅𐤄 pictographic Hebrew, the third character from right to left is the *Vav* 𐤅. The *Vav* represents the Holy Spirit in the gospel message. The Word of God has much to say about the power of the Holy Spirit in the believer's life. So when you draw out the picture of the *Vav* 𐤅 while sharing the gospel, remember the following points highlighted in John 14:26, "But the Helper, the Holy Spirit, whom the Father will send in My name, He will <u>teach you all things</u>, and bring to your remembrance all that I said to you."

First, who sent the Holy Spirit? None other than the Father by His giving right hand 𐤄. Second, in whose name did He send the Holy Spirit? None other than the Son, Jesus 𐤄—the salvation of 𐤉𐤄𐤅𐤄. Third, what will He do when you invite Him to take residence in your spirit? He will remind you, teach you, and give you power—the ability to fulfill your divine calling. Acts 1:8 tells us this clearly, "But you will receive power when the Holy Spirit has come upon you; and you shall be My witnesses both in Jerusalem, and in all Judea and Samaria, and even to the remotest part of the earth."

We have been created in the image of God and consist of three parts: body, soul, and spirit. The body is just a meat suit (flesh). Skin and bones. Jars of clay. The soul is a bit more mysterious. Biblically, the soul is referred to as the heart. In our modern society, the soul can also be referred to as the mind or psyche—the seat of our emotions, thoughts, and feelings. Our spirit, however, is a very different thing. For those of us who are born-again, our spirit is the perfect spirit of 𐤉𐤄𐤅𐤄. Our spirits are perfect and complete, bound eternally to 𐤉𐤄𐤅𐤄. For those outside of Christ, the spirit is disconnected from 𐤉𐤄𐤅𐤄. As an interesting side note, the picture of the gospel without you looks like this 𐤉𐤄𐤅. This is the exact image recently found at Mount Ebal in Israel. It was inscribed on the lead curse amulet. I see it as a picture of God without man.

The Word of God proclaims, "The heart is more deceitful than all else and is desperately sick; who can understand it?" (Jeremiah 17:9). The (heart/soul/psyche) is the middle ground between your flesh and your spirit. The heart is the place where trauma, pain, and childhood wounds accumulate. Your own sinful choices and the sinful choices of others gather here. It is a database of pain with a very large hard drive. This middle ground is where the battle is fought. On the one hand, we have the world, the flesh, and the sinful human nature that we all have pushing for its place in the heart. On the other hand, we have the powerful love of the Father seeking an intimate connection with our hearts. If you are not surrendered to and adopted by the Father, this is your biggest problem. Just like the curse amulet shows, because of sin you are disconnected from the Trinity. 𐤄 (you) . . . 𐤉𐤄𐤅 (the Trinity) . . . You have no power source! Nothing to plug into. Fix that first! Surrender and worship the Father, and receive His love through Jesus. Get adopted and receive the gift and power of the Holy Spirit 𐤉𐤄𐤅𐤄 (your adoption by the Trinity makes you complete). Only then will you have the power to unleash the fruit of the Spirit.

> [1] Therefore I urge you, brethren, by the mercies of God, to present your bodies a living and holy sacrifice, acceptable to God, *which is* your spiritual service of worship. [2] And do not be conformed to this world, but be transformed by the renewing of your mind, so that you may prove what the will of God is, that which is good and acceptable and perfect. Romans 12:1-2

Hidden in plain sight in the unspeakable name of God 𐤉𐤄𐤅𐤄 is the secret to victory (the gospel). The outstretched arms of the second *Hey*, surrendered and worshipping, model the posture one must assume to receive the power promised in Acts 1:8. The heart can only ever be truly healed through the power of the perfect Spirit of God 𐤉𐤄𐤅𐤄. When we surrender and worship, we use our will and choose to set our minds on the things of the Spirit. "For the mind set on the flesh is death, but the mind set on the Spirit is life and peace" (Romans 8:6). It is an act of your free will to set your mind on the things of the Spirit. It is your human nature to set your mind on the things of the flesh. The heart is the battleground. The heart is either filled up from the flesh (which is death) or from the Spirit (which is life and peace). God 𐤉𐤄𐤅𐤄 created you with a will, you will be lovingly welcomed but never forced or coerced. Living in a state of a renewed mind is your choice. Life and peace are yours through the willful act of surrender and worship. Have you received the perfect Spirit of God 𐤉𐤄𐤅𐤄? Would you like to?

When does the Holy Spirit come upon you? When you invite Him and receive Him in surrender and worship. What do you get? Adoption. You get welcomed into the throne room of Heaven as a joint heir with Jesus. What should you do? Worship and make disciples. Can you see that the name of God ✡Y✡﹄ is a picture of the gospel? If you need further convincing, consider Acts 2:33, which says, "Therefore having been exalted to the right hand of God, and having received from the Father the promise of the Holy Spirit, He has poured forth this which you both see and hear."

Who poured forth the Holy Spirit? He (the Holy Spirit) came through Jesus from the right hand of the Father. Where is Jesus? Exalted and at the right hand of the Father. Just like the picture shows. Look at Romans 8:9-11 again:

> [9] However, you are not in the flesh but in the Spirit, if indeed the Spirit of God dwells in you. But if anyone does not have the Spirit of Christ, he does not belong to Him. [10] If Christ is in you, though the body is dead because of sin, yet the spirit is alive because of righteousness. [11] But if the Spirit of Him who raised Jesus from the dead dwells in you, He who raised Christ Jesus from the dead will also give life to your mortal bodies through His Spirit who dwells in you.

Here we see the Holy Spirit referenced as both the Spirit of Christ and the Spirit of the Father ("Him who raised Jesus from the dead"). He is God, and He brings (drives deep) the power of God from Heaven down to you, securing you in Christ.

Now let's see what John 4:23 says about surrendering in worship through the Holy Spirit: "But an hour is coming, and now is, when the true worshipers will worship the Father in spirit and truth; for such people the Father seeks to be His worshipers." Who will we worship? The Father. How will we worship? In spirit and truth. Do you see yourself in the gospel? When the Father adopts you and gives you His Holy Spirit through the blood of His Son Jesus, you will worship because of this almost-too-good-to-be-true news. Your born-again spirit *needs* to worship 𐤉𐤄𐤅𐤄.

Why?

Every time you use the power of your free will to surrender and worship, you fulfill your destiny as a member of the Body of Christ—His Bride—the fully adopted child of God 𐤉𐤄𐤅𐤄. When you draw the second *Hey* 𐤄, you complete the name of God—you bring the whole concept down from Heaven. You are given the authority of the Godhead as evidenced by Matthew 16:19: "I will give you the keys of the kingdom of heaven; and whatever you bind on earth shall have been bound in heaven, and whatever you loose on earth shall have been loosed in heaven." This is how powerfully connected we are to the Trinity.

I present the idea that the name of God 𐤉𐤄𐤅𐤄 in pictographic Hebrew represents the gospel, and the gospel contains the keys to the Kingdom of Heaven. When you surrender to God and are adopted by the Father through Jesus, He binds you to Christ with His Spirit. This is a picture of the tent peg—the *Vav*. Your surrender to God 𐤉𐤄𐤅𐤄 means you are adopted by God 𐤉𐤄𐤅𐤄, not just on Earth but also in Heaven!

Consider the words of the apostle Paul in Ephesians 2:4-7:

> 4 But God, being rich in mercy, because of His great love with which He loved us, 5 even when we were dead in our transgressions, made us alive together with Christ (by

grace you have been saved), ⁶ and raised us up with Him, and seated us with Him in the heavenly places in Christ Jesus, ⁷ so that in the ages to come He might show the surpassing riches of His grace in kindness toward us in Christ Jesus.

You have been seated with Christ in heavenly places! The spiritual realm is unlike the natural realm—your spirit abides in Heaven right now, with יהוה in Christ Jesus. You are already seated there because your spirit is perfect in Jesus.

The news gets even better. When you're adopted and filled with the Holy Spirit, you don't just receive power; you receive *fruit*. Galatians 5:22-25 tells us:

> ²² But the fruit of the Spirit is love, joy, peace, patience, kindness, goodness, faithfulness, ²³ gentleness, self-control; against such things there is no law. ²⁴ Now those who belong to Christ Jesus have crucified the flesh with its passions and desires. ²⁵ If we live by the Spirit, let us also walk by the Spirit.

The Father has given you everything He has. You have all the fruit of the Holy Spirit within you. In surrender and worship, that fruit can flow from you to others, bringing the Love of the Father to this place at this time, fulfilling the gospel.

The Second Hey

Moving to the left of the *Vav*—the Holy Spirit—we now come to the second *Hey,* the final character in the name of God יהוה is *you*. The core message of the gospel is that God always intended to adopt you. He always intended for you to surrender and worship so you could receive and be filled with the power of His perfect Holy Spirit. Then by your own free will, you can loose God's love, plans, and purposes on Earth right now through the fruit of the Holy Spirit. You truly have the power (ability) to do that. It is your Father's will that you do that, and in so doing, you will fulfill the Great Commission found in Matthew 28.

Can you now see that the name of God 𐤄𐤅𐤄𐤉 in pictographic Hebrew is a diagram of the gospel? The Father 𐤄 sent His Son 𐤅, and through the Son, He sent His Spirit 𐤉. Through His Son and His Spirit, *He has adopted you* 𐤅 and seated you with Christ in heavenly places. The Spirit has given you power to share this astounding gospel with others and bear fruit for the Kingdom. The next time you need to share the gospel with someone, just draw them a picture of 𐤄𐤅𐤄𐤉 and explain to them what it means. The entire gospel is summed up in the simple name that God drew for Moses 3,500 years ago on top of a mountain. This is a gospel that you can stand on—a solid foundation for strengthening your faith.

A Diagram of God's Throne Room
within His Name

10.

Growing up in the Church during the seventies and eighties in rural Pennsylvania, my perception of God was that He was angry, vindictive, and outright scary. There was always some maladjusted youth pastor or camp counselor who would tell you that God would let you burn in hell forever if you were killed in a car accident on your way home from church without properly repenting. A host of creepy futuristic evangelical movies of the time, like A Thief in the Night[16] didn't help this picture of God as someone to be feared (and not in the good way).

These messages damaged the image I had of God deep in my soul. We were told we would all stand before God one day, where He would remind us of the sins we'd committed so we could weep and wail at the failures we had been in life. Later, however, while writing out my own copy of the book of Deuteronomy, I discovered an entirely different picture of my heavenly Father. I was transformed during this time and found that God is not vindictive and is certainly not waiting to burn people forever. I learned that God is, in fact, love; and frankly, when I read Deuteronomy, I realized God is way more fun than anyone ever gives Him credit for. I had to wonder, with so many scriptures describing His love, mercy, and kindness, how did the idea of God get so twisted by the Church?

Heaven is a very real place. Hear the words of Jesus from Matthew 6:9, "Pray, then, in this way: 'Our Father who is in heaven, hallowed be Your name.'" We will discuss this verse in detail in the next chapter on prayer but suffice it to say that Jesus Himself declares Heaven as the location of the Father. Heaven is where God is. The Greek word *ouranos*[17] used in the Matthew passage refers to the vaulted expanse where God dwells. In the Old Testament, the Hebrew word for Heaven is *šāmayim*[18], and is referenced 425 times. This word is also translated as "sky" in English versions. Again, it refers to the lofty sky, where God abides. Look at Genesis 21:17, where God deals gently with a harshly abused woman, "God heard the lad crying; and the angel of God called to Hagar from heaven and said to her, 'What is the matter with you, Hagar? Do not fear, for God has heard the voice of the lad where he is.'"

Heaven is where God abides, and there is a place for you there too.

Likewise, in Matthew 3:17, when Jesus is baptized in the Jordan, God the Father again speaks from Heaven, saying, "This is My beloved Son, in whom I am well-pleased." Before we move on and discuss the Tetragrammaton, allow me to share with you what I believe about Heaven. God is pure love, and Heaven is real. According to scripture, Heaven is where God abides—where the Father, the Son, and the Holy Spirit are seated in love and power—and as we have already discussed, there is a place for you there too.

There are many instances in scripture describing the throne room of Heaven, and we will go through some of them to gain insight into the specifics. Again, when reading the following passages, consider that the Tetragrammaton—the name of God ﬡﬢﬢﬡ in pictographic Hebrew—is a picture of the throne room of Heaven. As described by scripture, the orientation of the Trinity is clearly depicted. Note, too, that the word "LORD" in these passages refers to the Trinity—the full Godhead. Also, while reading these verses, remember that the throne room of God is a very real place and, as we shall see, a very *welcoming* place. As you read this chapter, if you are born again by the blood of Jesus and sealed by His Spirit, envision your spirit abiding there now.

Okay, let's start! Reading Job 1:6 provides a view into the *accessibility* of the throne room: "Now there was a day when the sons of God came to present themselves before the LORD, and Satan also came among them." This LORD that the writer of Job speaks of is the triune God, ﬡﬢﬢﬡ. I will avoid the rabbit trail of discussing who the sons of God were and focus on the fact that the triune God is approachable, even by the devil. If Satan himself came into the presence of the Trinity and questioned God, how much more should we, as God's children, enter boldly into His presence?

The prophet Micaiah presents us with another description of the throne room: "Micaiah said, 'Therefore, hear the word of the LORD. I saw the LORD sitting on His throne, and all the host of heaven standing on His right and on His left'" (2 Chronicles 18:18). The prophet saw the LORD ☥Y☥↲ (the Trinity) sitting in authority on the throne with the hosts of Heaven standing to the right and left. It is important to note that in this verse, LORD ☥Y☥↲ is plural, and the two instances of the word "His" have been inserted in the English translation and are not in the Hebrew text.

These verses tell us the triune LORD was seen sitting in authority on the throne, readily approachable. Now would be a good time to explain that in the rabbinical teaching style of Jesus, to teach while seated is to teach with authority. It is good for us to remember that God the Father is the ultimate authority. Psalms 9:7 tells us, "But the LORD abides forever. He has established His throne for judgment." The Hebrew word for judgment mentioned here is *mišpāṭ*[19] and concerns the act of deciding a legal case. We should then ask, "What kind of judge is God?" Deuteronomy 32:4 answers this question emphatically: "The Rock! His work is perfect, for all His ways are just; a God of faithfulness and without injustice, righteous and upright is He."

This passage tells us *that all God's ways are just*, and being just, God has provided every means for salvation and righteousness through His Son. The LORD is holy, and as such, He defines what is right, good, and true in the universe. The insight that the LORD abides forever and has established His throne for judgment provides a picture of God ✡Y✡⅃ as the origin of justice. This also shows that the throne room of Heaven is where justice was born and truth lives.

Psalms 89:14 explains the basis upon which God's throne rests: "Righteousness and justice are the foundation of Your throne; lovingkindness and truth go before You." *Lovingkindness*—there is that Hebrew word *chesed*[20] again, and it describes God beautifully. *This* is the God we serve. A God of justice and law rooted in the essential truth that God is love. Do you see it now? The throne room is not to be feared. This is where YHVH is. It is a place you want to be, in the lovingkindness—the *chesed*—of God where He not only requires justice but paid the price for the forgiveness of your sins.

2 Peter 3:9 makes it clear that God does not wish for any to perish but for all to come to repentance. God has predestined us to sonship by the blood of Jesus. God is love, and the throne room is a place of peace, safety, and love for the born-again believer. Jesus confirmed this when speaking to His disciples, assuring them there was a place for them in the throne room:

> And Jesus said to them, "Truly I say to you, that you who have followed Me, in the regeneration when the Son of Man will sit on His glorious throne, you also shall sit upon twelve thrones, judging the twelve tribes of Israel." Matthew 19:28

The writer of Hebrews takes it to the next level, telling us, "Therefore let us draw near with confidence to the throne of grace, so that we may receive mercy and find grace to help in time of need" (Hebrews 4:16). The writer encourages us to draw near to the throne room, not to cower in fear, but to enter in with confidence.

Faith Concepts Made Simple

When visualizing the pictographic Hebrew 𐤀𐤅𐤄𐤉 of the throne room, be mindful that the blood of Jesus predestined and paid for your place there: "Jesus, the author and perfecter of faith, who for the joy set before Him endured the cross, despising the shame, and has sat down at the right hand of the throne of God" (Hebrews 12:2). Your place in the throne room was made possible by the right hand of the Father, the outstretched arms of the Son, and the binding power of the Holy Spirit.

You have been adopted by God. A tent stake has been driven from the throne room into your spirit with power, binding you to the Godhead. When you are in Christ, you are complete, at peace with the Godhead, and entirely welcome to employ the power of the Holy Spirit. The picture of the born-again believer is of one who is welcome in the throne room, wholly eligible for grace, able to be broken, needy, and welcome at the same time.

When you look at the picture of God's name 𐤀𐤅𐤄𐤉 try to really *see* what it tells you. See the Father, the *Yod*, seated with His powerful right hand extended. See the *Hay*, the Son, seated to His right in power, arms outstretched in surrender to the *Yod* in payment for your access to the Trinity. See the Holy Spirit following Jesus and inside of you because you are in Christ, and He is in you. Jesus is sitting at peace and resting with the Father and you. The second *Hey* in God's name is a clear depiction of you and your place in the throne room as the adopted child of the Father.

When Stephen saw into the throne room just before the Council had him stoned, he described a slightly different picture: "But being full of the Holy Spirit, he gazed intently into heaven and saw the glory of God, and Jesus standing at the right hand of God" (Acts 7:55). The Greek word for God used here is *Theos* and is a reference to the Father—Jesus standing at the right hand of the Father. You may be thinking, *Now, wait a minute. In the other descriptions of the throne room, Jesus was seated at the right hand of the Father.* You would be correct, but let me explain how that scripture clearly depicts the throne room as a place of justice, lovingkindness, and divine awareness. This means our God is totally aware and fully engaged in our lives. Jesus witnessed Stephen's defense of the gospel, stood up in approval, and welcomed him into the throne room that day. How wonderful is that picture?

Jesus has made the same promise to us in Revelation 3:21, saying, "He who overcomes, I will grant to him to sit down with Me on My throne, as I also overcame and sat down with My Father on His throne." The throne room is a place to be anticipated for the born-again believer. The Word of God declares you an overcomer: "For whatever is born of God overcomes the

The throne room is a place to be anticipated for the born-again believer.

world; and this is the victory that has overcome the world—
our faith" (1 John 5:4). There's no talk of shame, anger, or
blame here. The throne room is a place of *chesed*, of divine
lovingkindness.

God Is Rich in Mercy

I have chosen but a small sampling of the scriptures related
to the throne room of Heaven. Study further and you'll be
even more assured that 3,500 years ago, when God gave His
true name to Moses ✶Υ✶⊐, He drew a picture of Himself in
His throne room. This picture of God's name plainly shows
the orientation of the components of the Trinity and the
adopted believer's subsequent position.

I want to close this chapter with a verse that means a
lot to me. Coming to an understanding of this verse literally
saved my life:

> [4] But God, being rich in mercy, because of His great love
> with which He loved us, [5] even when we were dead in our
> transgressions, made us alive together with Christ (by
> grace you have been saved), [6] and raised us up with Him,
> and seated us with Him in the heavenly places in Christ
> Jesus.
> Ephesians 2:4-6

This verse reminds me that I am adopted by the blood of
Jesus, that Jesus knows I will struggle in my flesh and in
my soul, but that my spirit is perfect. It also tells me a full
one-third of me is present and accounted for in the throne
room of Heaven right now.

I urge you to enjoy the truth of the Tetragrammaton
depicting the throne room of God while etching it on your

heart. Use your favorite Bible app to do a word study of the throne room of Heaven. In doing so, you will find the overwhelming message of God's love, your acceptance, and the Father's desire to return to *shalom* with His creation.

Also, next time a complex theological topic comes up in conversation, be bold and draw the pictographic Hebrew name of God 𐤉𐤄𐤅𐤄 on a napkin, a whiteboard, or a cardboard box if necessary. Or even pick up a stick and draw it in the dirt. Show the world that God is so kind and loving that He took the most difficult concepts of faith and drew a picture so simple that we could understand them.

The Flow of
Prayer

I was raised in a Christian home; we prayed about stuff. We prayed over meals, and we prayed when people were sick, traveling, or when we left the house for a trip. We prayed for missionaries, preachers, and ministries. My mom is a prayer warrior. I have more memories than I can count of seeing my mom on her knees talking to God. One time recently we had an outbreak of lice in our house. As you can imagine, it was not well received by a bunch of proper ladies with long flowing hair. As we stood flummoxed by the situation, my oldest daughter said, "I'm calling nana; she needs to pray about this!" "Therefore, confess your sins to one another, and pray for one another so that you may be healed. The effective prayer of a righteous man [nana] can accomplish much" (James 5:16). It turns out the lice problem was no match for God; it resolved quickly and in a delightful "only God" way.

What is prayer? In the pages of the Bible, prayer is defined as communicating in humility with God 𐤉𐤄𐤅𐤄. When we pray, at the heart of it, we believe that we can and are connecting to, and communicating with God 𐤉𐤄𐤅𐤄. In Matthew 6:5-8 Jesus has some powerful things to say about prayer:

> [5] When you pray, you are not to be like the hypocrites; for they love to stand and pray in the synagogues and on the street corners so that they may be seen by men. Truly I say to you, they have their reward in full. [6] But you, when you pray, go into your inner room, close your door and pray to your Father who is in secret, and your Father who sees *what is done* in secret will reward you. [7] And when you are praying, do not use meaningless repetition as the Gentiles do, for they suppose that they will be heard for their many words. [8] So do not be like them; for your Father knows what you need before you ask Him.

Jesus does not say, "If you decide to pray." He says, "When you pray." As born-again adopted believers, we are to be people of prayer. As you will come to see through this chapter, prayer is vital to the rhythm of our adoption. God is not ignorant of your life; God is in the know. God desires connection

As born-again adopted believers, we are to be people of prayer.

with you. You, my friend, are loved.

Jesus is about to explain to His disciples the flow of prayer. In Exodus 6:3, Moses is talking to God. The fact that Moses is having a literal conversation with God is astounding. Frankly, Moses is whining, and God is quite patient with him. In that moment, God reveals His true name to Moses YHWH. We have already seen that God's name YHWH is a diagram of the Trinity and the true gospel. Now Jesus is about to explain to us the flow of prayer. This flow is beautifully and simply modeled in the name of God YHWH. Luke 11:1 says: "It happened that while Jesus was praying in a certain place, after He had finished, one of His disciples said to Him, 'Lord, teach us to pray just as John also taught his disciples.'" Jesus' disciples ask Him for specific instructions regarding prayer. This is an excellent question, given that the disciples have seen the Pharisees and the teachers of the Law praying publicly (and likely dramatically) their whole lives. Jesus is different. The disciples see the difference, hear the difference, and have experienced the difference. Jesus steps right over the dogmas, legalism, and silliness and gets right to the heart of the matter. If we are going to renew our minds regarding prayer, Jesus is the right teacher.

Their rabbi (teacher) gives them the very best answer. In Matthew 6:9, Jesus begins His response by saying, "Pray, then, in this way: 'Our Father who is in heaven, hallowed be Your name.'" Did you catch it? Jesus starts this crucial instruction in the very same way the Tetragrammaton YHWH begins—*with the Father*. "Our Father" . . . there is an entire book wrapped up in just these two words "our Father." Notice that Jesus affirms our adoption when He refers to the Father as "our Father." Remember that God YHWH predestined us for adoption. Here, Jesus instructs His disciples to begin their prayer by directing their communication to the Father, ⅃ as "our Father." There is a flow to prayer. All love and power and blessing flow out of the Father. All petitions and praise from us must ultimately be directed to Him.

Jesus then affirms the location of our Father. He is in Heaven, in the throne room, seated in power and authority. Next, He says the most exciting part: "Hallowed be Your name." Do you see it? It has been right there in front of us for 3,500 years. God's name—ﭏYﭏ⅃—is hallowed (to make holy, to venerate) because it unlocks the Kingdom of God, the will of God, and the hope of mankind. In this instruction, it diagrams the model prayer Jesus offers. The name ﭏYﭏ⅃ begins with the Father, as does the model prayer. The flow of prayer begins with the surrendered and worshipping born-again believer ﭏ. Our born-again spirit needs to connect back to the Father. Like a lamp needs to be plugged into the socket so the power can flow and the light can shine, we too must plug into the love of God. So in surrender and praise, we begin our conversation with God. Our perfect born-again spirit is powerfully bonded to Christ by His blood sacrifice for us. As the Word of God says, He, Jesus ﭏ, sits in power next to His Father ⅃, our Father, and intercedes for us. Every prayer offered to the Father in the name of Jesus is hand-delivered. Through Jesus, your words land deep in the heart of the Father. He loves so enormously and so powerfully, and His perfect will responds. This flow is then directed back at you. The love of God, the blessing of God, and the will of God the Father is cast in your direction. This flow is through Christ and is delivered directly into your perfect born-again spirit through the Holy Spirit Y who lives inside you. When you look at the name of God ﭏYﭏ⅃ it all makes sense now. Everything the Father has flows right out of His "Righteous Right Hand" ⊢, and everything we send up flows left through the Holy Spirit Y.

Jesus continues in Matthew: 6:10: "Your kingdom come. Your will be done, on earth as it is in heaven." Yes, our Father has a will, and His will is *good*. Jesus gives clear evidence of this truth in Matthew 7:11: "If you then, being evil, know how to give good gifts to your children, how much more will your Father who is in heaven give what is good to those who ask Him!" The apostle Paul expands on this truth in Romans 12:2: "And do not be conformed to this world, but be transformed by the renewing of your mind, so that you may prove what the will of God is, that which is good and acceptable and perfect." Likewise, in Philippians 2:13, Paul says, "For it is God who is at work in you, both to will and to work for *His* good pleasure." Finally, in Hebrews 13:21, the writer says that God will "equip you in every good thing to do His will, working in us that which is pleasing in His sight, through Jesus Christ, to whom *be* the glory forever and ever. Amen." We want His will to be done. I have lived long enough now, and I've done it my way enough times to know that His way is always better. Somehow in the religion and rules of church, we got convinced that God is mean and not to be trusted. This could not be farther from the truth because the Father is pure love.

We know the Father ⊢ is working in us through Jesus ⵣ and the Holy Spirit Y. He has driven His power, His authority, and His salvation down from Heaven deep into us, His adopted children, because we have responded to Him. In Heaven, created angelic beings worship and serve the Godhead of their free will. On Earth, the same thing is true of the born-again believer. So Jesus teaches us to pray that God's good will is done here on Earth as it is in Heaven. How will God's ✡Y✡⅃ will be done? It will be done on Earth as it is in Heaven through the surrendered, worshiping born-again believer by the power of the Holy Spirit. The fruit of the Holy Spirit flows out of the surrendered and worshipping believer ✡. "But the fruit of the Spirit is love, joy, peace, patience, kindness, goodness, faithfulness, gentleness, self-control; against such things there is no law" (Galatians 5:22-23). There is, however, tangible resistance to God's will on this planet.

How do the adopted sons and daughters operate in God's ✡Y✡⅃ will, bringing it from Heaven to Earth, despite the raging spiritual war? Ephesians 6:11-12 gives us the answer:

> [11] Put on the full armor of God, so that you will be able to stand firm against the schemes of the devil. [12] For our struggle is not against flesh and blood, but against the rulers, against the powers, against the world forces of this darkness, against the spiritual *forces* of wickedness in the heavenly *places*.

The struggle is real, and prayer is the communication strategy the Father has ordained for us to surrender and worship in His direction. We then receive manifold blessings and power from His direction, empowering us to accomplish His good will on Earth. This continual flow of power between God and us is what makes the light shine! "Let your light shine before men in such a way that they may see your good works, and glorify your Father who is in heaven" (Matthew 5:16). It is your light! You decide to let it shine. When you do, when you surrender 𝍢 and worship 𝍢 the Father ⨆ through Jesus 𝍢 and the power of the Holy Spirit Y . . . *Kaboom!* On it comes.

Jesus continues in Matthew 6:11: "Give us this day our daily bread." Have you ever wondered why Jesus instructs us to ask that our Father give us *daily* bread? It is because anything more will reduce our dependency on God. Our bread is given daily because we need to remain in constant contact and communion with our Father. If the Father gave us weekly bread, monthly bread, yearly bread, or even worse, if He gave us a lifetime

Our bread is given daily because we need to remain in constant contact and communion with our Father.

supply of bread all at once, we would end up in a place where we might forget how desperately we need Him. Remember the lessons of Deuteronomy? Deuteronomy is the book that started this whole journey. Deuteronomy inspired the book you are reading. The entire book of Deuteronomy can be summarized in a few simple words: "Don't forget Me, don't forget Me, *please* don't forget Me!" God wants to be with us; that has been the desire from the beginning. If you look at God's name 𝍢Y𝍢⨆, you are in it. The Father has always wanted to adopt you and bring you back into the family.

Next, in Matthew 6:12, Jesus says, "And forgive us our debts, as we also have forgiven our debtors." This part is so powerful! First, remember that Jesus is directing this prayer to the Father, and the Father has the power to forgive. Next, do you recall the picture of the *Yod* ﬥ casting or throwing? Let's see what Psalms 103:12 says, "As far as the east is from the west, so far has He removed our transgressions from us." Isn't that beautiful? When we repent, God casts our sins as far as the east is from the west. "If we confess our sins, He is faithful and righteous to forgive us our sins and to cleanse us from all unrighteousness" (1 John 1:9). That means God removes and forgets our sins *permanently*.

Here comes the best part—as we are forgiven, we can now mimic our Father's behavior and bring Heaven to Earth *by forgiving others*. Ephesians 5:1 says, "Therefore be imitators of God, as beloved children." We forgive because we are called to mimic our Abba (Father) as His adopted children. This image takes us right back to the pictographic name of God ﭏﬥ. We seek forgiveness from Him, and as He freely forgives us, so we must usher His forgiveness into the world. It is crucial we forgive. It is vital to remove the cycle of sin and offense because we are called to imitate our heavenly Father. The issue of forgiveness is so vital to maintaining the flow of power between God and us that Jesus offers this dire warning in Matthew 6:14-15: "For if you forgive others for their transgressions, your heavenly Father will also forgive you. But if you do not forgive others, then your Father will not forgive your transgressions." This is not the Father being mean; this is a spiritual reality as true as gravity. If you don't forgive, your own forgiveness and connection are

> *The issue of forgiveness is vital to maintaining the flow of power between us and God.*

interrupted. Forgiveness is hard, real hard sometimes, but don't mess with the flow.

When we know what we're looking for in this model prayer, we can again see the message of the pictographic Hebrew name of God—𐤄𐤅𐤄𐤉. As I've shown, the name of God is a diagram for how prayer works, made so simple you can draw it with a pencil on a Post-it note. It is a message that can be understood by children, teens, adults, and even people who don't speak your language. It is a message that is profoundly simple yet eternally deep. It is rooted in the universal pre-Genesis 11 language and communication of mankind. The Father gives and blesses from His right hand 𐤉, and the Son 𐤄 receives from the Father and transmits blessing and power through the Holy Spirit 𐤅 directly into the spirit of the adopted born-again believer 𐤄. The born-again (surrendered and worshipping) believer brings Heaven to Earth when the love of the Father is made manifest in your daily life by the power of the human free will, which is set on the things of the Spirit. "For those who are according to the flesh set their minds on the things of the flesh, but those who are according to the Spirit, the things of the Spirit. For the mind set on the flesh is death, but the mind set on the Spirit is life and peace" (Romans 8:5-6). Who doesn't want life and peace? The free will choice to "set your mind" on the Spirit is tough, but it's your choice to make. If you do, the benefits are guaranteed and profound.

The pathway of prayer for the born-again believer is the same in reverse. This is why surrendering to the love of God through Jesus is so vitally important. There is no path to the Father but through Jesus. "Jesus said to him,

'I am the way, and the truth, and the life; no one comes to the Father but through Me'" (John 14:6). The adopted born-again believer approaches the Father with prayer. "Be anxious for nothing, but in everything by prayer and supplication with thanksgiving let your requests be made known to God" (Philippians 4:6). In these moments, we as believers approach our Father freely and without fear, as a child approaches a loving parent with a need or concern. The Holy Spirit inside us is connected directly to Jesus, who intercedes for us and communicates our requests directly to the Father on our behalf. We literally have a direct line into the heart of God the Father through the blood of Jesus and the indwelling Holy Spirit. If you need more evidence, look at 1 John 2:1, "My little children, I am writing these things to you so that you may not sin. And if anyone sins, we have an Advocate with the Father, Jesus Christ the righteous." Similarly, 1 Timothy 2:5 says, "For there is one God, *and* one mediator also between God and men, *the* man Christ Jesus." This level of connection is simply not available to those outside the Spirit of God "because the mind set on the flesh is hostile toward God; for it does not subject itself to the law of God, for it is not even able *to do so*, and those who are in the flesh cannot please God" (Romans 8:7-8). Take the leap. Surrender to the love of the Father today. Invite His Spirit to abide in you. Seek His adoption through the blood of Jesus. Receive His Holy Spirit into your Spirit and receive power.

God's Name as a
Tool for Evangelism

Jesus said in Matthew 28:19, "Go therefore and make disciples of all the nations, baptizing them in the name of the Father and the Son and the Holy Spirit." We make disciples by walking, talking, and doing life with people. God first modeled this in the garden of Eden with Adam and Eve. Jesus continues this model by walking, talking, and doing life with His disciples. Introducing, and sometimes re-introducing people to the love of God should be at the root of any evangelism effort. "Or do you think lightly of the riches of His kindness and tolerance and patience, not knowing that the kindness of God leads you to repentance?" (Romans 2:4). The repentance Paul speaks of here refers to the "changing of one's mind." This understanding of repentance is key for evangelism. God gave all of us our own will; we are free to "set our mind" on whatever it is that we decide to do. Getting exposed to and informed about the love of God is key to changing our mind. "How then will they call on Him in whom they have not believed? How will they believe in Him whom they have not heard? And how will they hear without a preacher?" (Romans 10:14).

Many of us, myself included, were raised in the church and taught either implicitly or explicitly that God is mean, cold, and vengeful. Many of us, myself included, had a moment where we had to "repent"—to "change our mind"—about the very nature of God. My study of the name of God led me to conclude that God (the Trinity) is way more loving and way more fun than anyone gives Him credit for. My firm conviction is that the gospel message in its purest form is well represented in the pictographic Hebrew name of God 𐤉𐤄𐤅𐤄. Using the name of God 𐤉𐤄𐤅𐤄 as a primary evangelism tool allows us to share the gospel with people of all walks of life, cultures, and ages. It truly allows us to start at the beginning. It is the very best place to start.

I believe that it is a worthwhile endeavor to question what our real aim is when we evangelize. Are we focused on works, or are we evangelizing out of guilt or under the compulsion of others? Is it a pride thing, or are we just looking for numbers to post and a badge to wear? Over the years, I have been involved in various evangelistic outreaches, with elements of all these present. I spent some time working with a group of folks who would just put up a tent and wait for people to walk in and ask questions about God. This straightforward, straight-up engagement was the most effective I have ever seen, though I'm sure there are others. I would go out on a limb and say that most born-again believers are simply unprepared when the moment arises. I will make the case that sharing the love of God by showing people what His name looks like and what it means is a simple and powerfully engaging method. Of course, it is not the only method by any means, but one worth considering.

A Few Words about "Fear-Based" Evangelism

In the early years of our marriage, my wife and I attended a fundamentalist church where the classic "turn or burn" approach was very common. In this method of evangelism, you focus on the fear of God and the wrath of God. There is an abundance of spiritual manipulation. People are coerced, pressured, and essentially scared into robotically repeating some pre-scripted prayer. Have you ever heard someone use the strategy, "If you don't repent right now, you could die in the car on your way home, be separated from your family, and burn in hell forever"? Let me stop and ask you a very simple question. How many of your loving, meaningful, and stable relationships are based on fear and manipulation? I hope, for your sake, the answer is zero. Fear and manipulation are not the way to introduce people to the love of God. This type of evangelism can leave lasting scars and misconceptions about the goodness of God. I am sure that there are many well-meaning people out there who have used these methods. As mature born-again believers, we must resist this.

It's Tough to Start in the Middle

During our time at the fundamentalist church, we had some missionaries serving with New Tribes Mission in Central America stay with our congregation for a few months. This is when I first became aware of the struggles missionaries encounter when sharing the gospel. They told us how they had to completely abandon their evangelism strategy, which started in the New Testament. They found it challenging to share the gospel with tribal people because there was just too much backstory to overcome. Over time I came to find out that it wasn't just tribal people groups that had this struggle. People from all walks of life, age groups, and cultures struggle to comprehend the gospel when we start the story in the middle. Hopefully, when you picked this book up, you opened to the front, read the Introduction, started in Chapter One, and worked your way to the end. This makes perfect sense when reading a book, and it makes perfect sense when sharing the gospel as well. In general, people will have a much easier time when we start at the beginning.

Simple Evangelism That Works

The Tetragrammaton 𐤉𐤄𐤅𐤄 resonates with all humans at an origin level. I have studied this name for over fourteen years. When I started, I had never seen it before, but it called to me on a very deep level. This name predates race, ethnicity, and most everything that separates and divides us as humans. Most modern evangelicals have never seen the Tetragrammaton, don't understand it, and it is not an arrow in their quiver. There is even less of a chance that you will find a person who is not born-again that has any idea what they are looking at. This is good news! Most people love a good story, and the name of God 𐤉𐤄𐤅𐤄 is a diagram of a *very* good story.

Once you see it, you can't unsee it. When you draw the Tetragrammaton 𐤉𐤄𐤅𐤄 and begin to tell the story, people quickly become fascinated because, let's face it, you're literally looking at how God wrote His own name. The beauty of using the Tetragrammaton for evangelism is that all you do is draw a picture and explain what it means. Hopefully, the first eight chapters of this book have given you what you will need to

The Tetragrammaton resonates with all humans at an origin level.

draw, explain, and share the very best story of all.

Okay, Let's See What This Looks Like Practically

If you want to tell a good story, the very best place to start is at the beginning. "In the beginning, God" is how the Bible begins. In my day job, I have learned the power of asking the right questions. Evangelism is no different. When you ask the logical question, "Who is God?" this allows you to introduce the God of the Bible 𐤉𐤄𐤅𐤄. For example, the personal, intimate name of God shows up in Genesis 2:4, "This is the account of the heavens and the earth when they were created, in the day that the LORD God made earth and heaven." Use this verse to explain who the "LORD" is 𐤉𐤄𐤅𐤄. Explain that since the very beginning of civilization, false gods have been on the scene. It is powerful to make the distinction that the LORD 𐤉𐤄𐤅𐤄 is the singular, real deal. There is none like Him or beside Him.

Draw the picture 𐤉𐤄𐤅𐤄. Don't waste any time getting the name of God in front of your listener. When you draw the picture, you set yourself up for a clear presentation. You give yourself placeholders, and you provide the listener with a concrete reference for the things you are telling them. Remember, pictographic Hebrew is rooted in the concrete. The western mind is trained to think in the abstract. Being able to look at a picture of the name of God will likely be a significant first for most people. Once you have the picture, you can start asking questions. Have you ever seen this before? How do you feel when you look at it? Did you know that your life and future are accounted for in this picture? Would you like me to explain it to you? If you will indulge me, I'll give you a short example of what this would have looked like if someone had shared it with me twenty years ago.

> Old Me: I have really been struggling in my relationship with God. He feels so distant to me. I was raised in the Church, and at this point in my life, I should be at peace with these truths. Still, I seem to be struggling more now than ever before.

> New Me: I have something cool to show you related to this topic. So if I were to draw a simple picture of how you feel right now, would it look like this? This is you . . . 𐤅 and this is God . . . 𐤉𐤄𐤅𐤄, and you are feeling disconnected.

> Old Me: Uh, yeah. That is a really weird way to describe it, but it pretty much nails how I'm feeling right now. I get the me picture, but where did the picture of God come from?

New Me: So what I drew for you is actually something God drew for Moses about 3,500 years ago when Moses was having a bit of a spiritual crisis himself. Except when God drew it for Moses, it looked a little different, like this ✲Υ✲⌐. This is the name of God in pictographic Hebrew, and believe it or not, it holds the key to solving your crisis the same way it did for Moses. If I can have three to five minutes, I'll explain it to you.

Old Me: Well, the crisis has been brewing for thirty years, and I have started to feel hopeless, so yes, I can devote three to five minutes to getting it solved.

New Me: Sweet, here it goes. First, you read pictographic Hebrew from right to left. The first character, the thing that looks like a right arm, that's the *Yod* ⌐. The reason it looks like a right arm is because that is what it is; it represents the Father. It is a picture of His creating, giving, and sending nature. The second character, the man with his arms stretched out, that is the *Hey* ✲. This character represents Jesus, the second Person of the Trinity who came down here and became one of us. He lived a perfect life and willingly sacrificed Himself on a Roman cross to give us salvation. The third character, the one that looks like the letter Y, it's a picture of a tent stake. This is the *VAV* Υ. The *VAV* represents the third Person of the Trinity, the Holy Spirit. This is the same Holy Spirit that God sent to live inside us after Jesus was resurrected from the dead. Just like a tent stake holds a tent down in heavy winds, the Holy Spirit locks you fast to God. He also provides direct access to the Father through Jesus, twenty-four seven.

Old Me: Whoa, that is cool! I have been a Christian for thirty years. Why didn't anyone ever show me this before? I love it. It makes so much sense, but I do have some questions. There are three Persons in the Trinity.

I have been taught that my whole life, so who is the fourth person? Also, why is it so hard for me to feel loved by God? When I was a kid, they scared me into saying a "sinners' prayer." I did it because I didn't want to go to Hell. I have spent thirty years trying to follow the rules and feeling like garbage when I failed.

New Me: Yeah, me too. You are in good company feeling this way. There are a lot of us in this camp. Let me start by answering your first question, and then the second one will hopefully answer itself. God is the one who chose to give Himself a four-character name. He did this because He is perfect love. The secret of the name of God is that the fourth *Hey* 𐤄 is you! Do you remember having to memorize John 3:16 as a kid? "For God so loved the world." God the Father is one hundred percent love. Front to back, top to bottom, pure love. You see, the Bible talks about our "adoption" a lot. God the Father has always wanted to adopt you. He never wanted you to be scared into His family. He wanted you to be loved into His Kingdom. Every time you look at the name of God, you are reminded that your destiny has always been to be adopted by God. It has always been about love, not fear.

Old Me: Wait a minute, are you suggesting that God is not mad at me? This has been the root of my faith since I was a little boy. What about all those stories of God wiping out entire groups of people?

New Me: Yep, that's what I'm telling you. God is not mad at you. God gave Adam and Eve free will. He let them think for themselves, to choose for themselves. They chose to sin and broke the sweet connection they enjoyed with God. Because of this choice, God made His own choice to send His own Son down to Earth to become one of us so that the sweet connection between

God and man could be restored. You told me that you feel like garbage when you fail; God knew you would fail. First John 1:8 says that we all sin, all of us. That is why we needed a Savior. Your sin is no great shock to God; He knows all about it.

Old Me: Yeah, but I'm still a little hung up on how a loving God can allow so much pain and suffering in the world. I mean, He did take a hard stance against various people groups throughout history.

New Me: True, but can you think of any Bible stories where God just randomly gets angry? God is pure love, and every time in the scriptures that God punishes mankind, it is always in response to the sinful free will choices they have made and the impact those choices have on the innocent. If someone thwarts a mass shooter, we don't call them a murderer; we call them a hero. The hard truth is that God gave you free will and lets you choose to love Him or not. God does not force anyone to love Him or to accept the salvation of Jesus. If there is no freedom to choose, there is no love. Free will is the most dangerous thing in the universe, and many people have made some pretty poor choices. Often times these choices impact the innocent; this is the point where the wrath of God comes into play. The Bible clearly states that the "wages of sin is death." When you choose to sin, you choose a path that ends in death.

Old Me: I can see that. I see people in my life, and even myself making poor choices every day. So how do we get off the hamster wheel of poor choices?

New Me: That, my friend, is the essence of the gospel. You make a good choice; you choose the love of God. You surrender to the love God displayed for you through the sacrifice of Jesus on the cross. The reason the picture of you in the name of God is that of a person with their hands up is because your adoption by God the Father starts when you surrender to His love for you. As soon as you do, He forgives you, and He fills you with His Holy Spirit which gives you power. As soon as you get the Holy Spirit, your hands go right back up in praise and worship. This surrender and adoption are how it all begins for you. Over time, as you continue to surrender and He continues to give you power, you become more and more and more like the Father. The fruit of love, joy, and peace flow out of you more and more. Your faith grows, and your connection to God is locked fast by the Holy Spirit.

Old Me: I can see it now; I feel disconnected because I am. Many of the things I have believed about God are just plain wrong. I have always struggled to feel that God loves me. I have always connected my performance with His acceptance of me.

New Me: I know, I lived there too. God knew you could not measure up, and that is why He sent Jesus. The Bible says that your adoption is a free gift of God's love, not something you earn. When Jesus talks about being born-again, this choice to accept the love of God and be adopted as His child is what He is talking about. You are either born-again and adopted, or you aren't. God will never make you choose Him, but His very name declares boldly that He chose you 𐤉𐤄𐤅𐤄.

This was an abbreviated discussion based on my own life experience. I am sure other people will have other questions, objections, and struggles but it gives you foundation from which to discuss the concept. Through the entire discussion, I was able to stand on the truth that is baked into the name of God 𐤉𐤄𐤅𐤄, and so can you.

The Tetragrammaton for Kids

When we teach children about God, the first thing they need to know about is the love of God. Most kids like to draw pictures, and they love a good story. What an amazing God we have, and even more amazing is that He revealed Himself to Moses in a picture that a child can understand. Kids are quick; once you draw them this picture and explain it to them, they will waste no time showing it to other kids.

A while back, I gave a talk to a group of men, and one man brought his five-year-old daughter with him. Frankly, the kiddo didn't have anywhere else to go, so she sat there quietly and listened as I shared the same gospel message I'm sharing with you now. A few days later at a doctor's appointment, the lady doctor walked out and told her

When we teach children about God, the first thing they need to know about is the love of God.

dad that this little girl had just boldly shared the gospel with her using the pictographic Hebrew (I guess she hadn't met many five-year-olds who knew about pictographic Hebrew). It was so simple it stuck, and the doctor was shocked.

If you find it difficult to share the gospel with adults, try explaining the Trinity and adoption to a child. This is where the beautiful simplicity of a picture comes in. When you see the response children have, I can almost guarantee it will generate confidence in you to begin sharing with others. So how do you explain the gospel to a child using the Tetragrammaton? Let me provide an example of how this conversation may go.

Have you ever seen the picture of God's name? Would you like me to draw it for you? 𐤉𐤅𐤄𐤉 Pretty cool, huh? Would you like me to explain it? Look here. It was written in Hebrew, and we read Hebrew from right to left, so we start with this picture. This thing that looks like an arm is the *Yod* character, and that represents God the Father. The reason it's drawn as an arm is that the Father always gives, always blesses, and always loves His children. Did you know God the Father loves you more than you can ever imagine? It is true! He does.

Next, you have this second picture, this guy with his arms stretched out. This character is called the *Hey*. Have you heard God the Father has a Son named Jesus? Did you know that Jesus left Heaven and became a man who lived here on Earth for a while? Jesus was killed on a Roman cross to save all of us. This is why He is shown with His arms stretched out. Did you know that three days later, He rose from the dead and then went up to Heaven and that He is still alive in Heaven, preparing a beautiful home just for you? Obviously, Jesus loves you too!

Yeah, this third picture is a weird one. It is a tent peg. It is called the *Vav*. Have you ever seen or helped your parents put up a tent? Tent pegs keep the tent from blowing away in the wind. Remember that God sent Jesus to Earth to live here for a while? Did you know that after Jesus was raised from the dead and then went to Heaven, God sent His very own Spirit to live inside us and to help us? Just like a tent peg keeps a tent from blowing away, God's Spirit places His love right inside us and keeps us joined fast to God.

Now look at this fourth picture! Yeah, did you notice that too? It is another person, just like the other one with his arms stretched out. Can you lift your hands and stretch them out like this? Do you see it? This is a picture of you! God the Father has always wanted to adopt you as His child. The reason Jesus, the Son of God, came to Earth was to make it possible for you to be adopted. Then once you get adopted, God sends a special gift into your heart and spirit to live there and help you. This is His Holy Spirit we spoke about earlier. The only thing we have to do to be adopted by God is to ask Him. Just lift your hands like in this picture and tell God you're sorry for the times you chose to do the wrong things. Ask Him to please adopt you through Jesus and have His Spirit come and live in your heart. Because He loves you and wants to adopt you into His family, He does.

The reason our hands are lifted up in the picture is to show us what to do. You see, the first time we lift them up is to give in to God and tell Him that we choose Him. Then, as soon as we do, He gives us His Spirit, and we lift our hands back up to show God how happy and thankful we are that His Holy Spirit lives inside us. Would you like God to adopt you as His child and send His Spirit to live in you and help you?

Children who see and understand God's love and plan for adoption in His name are far more open to receiving His salvation (Jesus). Frightening children into the Kingdom of God never creates secure, effective disciples. It is a very bad idea to attempt to manipulate children into the Kingdom with talk of God's wrath and His anger. The irony of this misguided strategy is that the only time the Father ever displays wrath and anger is in the face of injustice and unrighteousness. Nothing invokes the wrath of the Father quicker than the harming of innocent children. We must always begin where the name of God begins ࠉࠄࠅࠄ, with the pure love of the Father.

Make Disciples of All the Nations

Sharing God's love with people who speak different languages than you using the Tetragrammaton is simple and enjoyable, too. You might only be able to speak their language brokenly, but you can draw the picture and tell them the story. Begin with what we discussed about what most cultures have in common—the story of the flood, the Tower of Babel, pictographic writing, and pyramids. Share the story of Moses and the children of Israel. Explain how the name of God is also the name of Jesus and that God came to Earth to save them.

Using the Tetragrammaton to share God's love with people who speak a different language is simple and enjoyable.

Tell them the Father loves them, and they can be forgiven and adopted. Describe how they can receive the Holy Spirit and live free forever in Christ, starting immediately.

I once shared this message in the little country church where my grandma worshipped. They invite me to preach occasionally, and I enjoy going there. I wanted to teach them about the name of God 𐤉𐤄𐤅𐤄, the throne room, and the adoption of the born-again believer. As I considered my options, I had a moment of inspiration. I drove to the hardware store and purchased four white folding chairs and a couple of paint pens for about thirty bucks. I took them to my shop, and I carefully painted each chair to display the characters of the Tetragrammaton. Then I really got creative. I painted flow arrows on the chairs showing the direction of the Father's will, love, and blessing. I showed a flow arrow on the second *Hey* chair diagramming the route our prayers take to the heart of the Father. The chairs for the Holy Spirit and for Jesus had flow arrows that went both ways. Our prayers flow through them on the way up, and the Father's love and blessing flow through them on the way back down. These chairs looked awesome, and I was quite proud of myself.

I shared the gospel that Sunday morning, and it went really well. It gave people something to look at while I described the name of God ﬩Y﬩﬩. As I shared, I would sit in each of the chairs as I described the role and meaning. When I got to the chair for the second *Hey*, it gave me a chance to ask them some questions. Have you chosen the adoption of the Father? Have you accepted your seat in the throne room of Heaven? When you look in the mirror, do you see the adopted child of God? Is the power of the Holy Spirit jacking you up on the inside every day? Are you experiencing the power and peace of the Holy Spirit daily in your life?

These are hard questions if you have to answer no. However, the chair is open to everyone, and if you are so bold as to ask, you can even invite people to come forward and try it out. Pointing to each chair, say, "Here's the Father, here's the Son, here's the Holy Spirit, and check this out . . . this is *your* seat! Would you like to come and sit in this chair?" So many people have been conditioned to strive that the idea of sitting down in the place God has for you and resting is almost crazy talk. Through the love of God, however, it is possible to "rest forward"—to choose the love of the Father, to sit down and enjoy His adoption and the power of His Holy Spirit, then rise and live big out of the overflow of the love and power of God.

To my Christian brothers and sisters, I have shared every drop of my revelation and research with you. I have endeavored to show the deep truths of God embedded in the picture of His name. My hope for you is that you find encouragement and motivation to press on. My prayer for you is that this information strengthens your faith and provides new avenues for growth and tools for sharing the love of God in Christ Jesus with the world. I pray that you "set your mind" on things of the Spirit. Above all, I pray the power of God and the supernatural inspiration of His Holy Spirit rises inside you and produces great fruit. We live in unprecedented times, and the Kingdom of God is very near.

A Closing Appeal to Our Jewish Brothers and Sisters

I close this book somewhat uniquely because I strongly sense that most readers will be Christians or seekers looking to deepen their faith. I have lived my entire adult life as a passionate Zionist. I have a deep and abiding love for the people and the land of Israel, the root of which is nothing less than divine. My soul is alive when my feet walk the dusty paths of the Bible. I love to sit along the Sea of Galilee and watch the sun set over Tiberias. I received my filling of the Holy Spirit while standing broken in the Jordan River. I close with an impassioned plea for my dear Jewish brothers and sisters to consider the revelations inside this book. I implore you to take a hard look at God's pictographic Hebrew name and see *Messiah*. Consider for a moment that Moses truly did declare the triune nature of God 𐤅𐤉𐤅𐤄.

I ask that you consider the word selection of Moses in the use of *Elohim.* I ask that you consider the words of Isaiah 45:17, "Israel has been saved by the LORD with an everlasting salvation; you will not be put to shame or humiliated to all eternity." I ask that you consider the truth that the name of Jesus Himself literally means "the salvation of 𐤉𐤄𐤅𐤄." I ask that you consider the words of Isaiah 7:14, "Therefore the Lord Himself will give you a sign: Behold, a virgin will be with child and bear a son, and she will call His name Immanuel." Where in the history of humanity is there such a compelling fulfillment of this prophecy than in the birth of Jesus?

Finally, I ask that you consider the words of the Apostle Paul, Pharisee of Pharisees, born a Benjamite, circumcised on the eighth day, raised at the feet of Gamaliel. I yield the final words of this book to Paul and his letter to the church in Rome. I put my full heart alongside his in this moment. You, dear friends, are deeply loved.

> [1] I am telling the truth in Christ, I am not lying, my conscience testifies with me in the Holy Spirit, [2] that I have great sorrow and unceasing grief in my heart. [3] For I could wish that I myself were accursed, *separated* from Christ for the sake of my brethren, my kinsmen according to the flesh, [4] who are Israelites, to whom belongs the adoption as sons, and the glory and the covenants and the giving of the Law and the *temple* service and the promises, [5] whose are the fathers, and from whom is the Christ according to the flesh, who is over all, God blessed forever. Amen.
> Romans 9:1-5

About the Author

Gregory Martz is a family man, technology entrepreneur, Bible teacher and lover of Israel. He is the founder of Martz Technologies, VZRscada, Clean PA, and the Men of the Land Podcast. Gregory is a Christ-follower with a passion for family, community and philanthropy. He holds degrees in Electronics Engineering and Integrated Ministry. Gregory and his family reside in Berwick, Pennsylvania.

Endnotes

1   Tomlin, Chris. Good Good Father. Sixsteps Records, October 2, 2015.

2   Strong's G2962 – *kyrios*

3   IBID

4   Transliteration definition & meaning (no date) Dictionary.com. Dictionary.com. Available at: https://www.dictionary.com/browse/transliteration (Accessed: February 17, 2023).

5   Strong's G2424 – *iēsous*

6   Strong's H3091 – *yᵊhôšûaʿ*

7   Strong's H8527 - *talmîḏ*

8   Strong's H2009 – *hinneh*

9   Strong's H7307 – *ruah*

10   Strong's G4151 - *pneuma*

11   Strong's H3027 – *yāḏ*

12   Strong's H2389 – *ḥāzāq*

13   Strong's H7965 – *shalom*

14   Strong's G2098 – *euangelion*

15   Strong's H2617 – *chesed*

16   A Thief in the Night (1972). United States: Mark IV Pictures.

17   Strong's G3772 – *ouranos*

18   Strong's H8064 – *šāmayim*

19   Strong's H4941 – *mišpāṭ*

20   Strong's H2617 – *chesed*